The Faces of Music

THE FACES of MUSIC

A Salem-Keizer Connection

FRANK SPRAGG

LUMINARE PRESS
WWW.LUMINAREPRESS.COM

The Faces of Music: A Salem-Keizer Connection

Printed in the United States of America

Cover Design: Claire Flint Last

Luminare Press
442 Charnelton St.
Eugene, OR 97401
www.luminarepress.com

ISBN: 978-1-64388-089-1
LOC: 2019937213

To my wife, Judith Spragg

Table of Contents

Author's Note

THIS BOOK WAS ORIGINALLY INTENDED TO BE THE LAST chapter of a larger book, *Face the Music Education: The Great Salem-Keizer School Distric Music Program*, which I am publishing simultaneously. The information combined in one book was so voluminous that my publisher suggested that this work and *Face the Music Education* be separate. This is a logical choice. Within this book is information that may or may not be related to *Face the Music Education* and stands well on its own.

Foreword

Pat yourself on the back. Cry from the housetops. With little effort you will have compiled a list as good as mine. And you should. Every human on this planet is influenced by music in some form, some to a profound degree. They are crawling toward you, grasping at your ankles, pleading to be on your list. So promote them. They deserve it.

Despite the acclaim you will receive, I consider my list exceptional. I have approached people who were influenced by music in all manner of ways. My collection is unfocused and this is by design. Music, in whatever path it takes, is essential to us all.

In that spirit, I sought a wide range of scenarios: people who have been influenced by music or have influenced others, via career, avocation, or in life. In some cases, music has helped people be successful in a life unrelated to music. For others, music has been a passion throughout their lives. And for still others, the influence has been incidental but crucial.

My initial plan was to spotlight people who were *saved* by music. However, I soon understood this target was too narrow, that it represented a small fraction of people who have benefited from music. I know of one woman whose education gave her a career in music but whose personal life remains a mess. I therefore broadened the list to include those who were *changed* by music. But this still was not the right fit. As Ben Stokes, band director at South High School in Salem, Oregon reminded me, some of us have a passion for music from the day we were born.

My list can't include just those who most deserve to be on it. Who most deserves to be on my list? My older sister, Sheila, and her husband, Mike, once took a long trip around the western United States, arriving one evening at a hamlet on the border of Oregon and Nevada. They asked the proprietor of the only store in town where they might camp for the night. Looking at the surrounding desert and with a sweep of his hand, he said, "There's a million acres out there. Have at it." Which acre was most suitable? You tell me. Each acre represents a person most deserving to be on my list.

I finally settled on the word *impacted*—those who have been impacted by music. By no means are all the people on my list from Salem or Keizer. I aimed for variety wherever that might lead. In accomplishing this, some of the stories I heard were from people I had not previously considered. But I am pleased with what I discovered.

Cheyenne Dunne Hayes

Cheyenne loved choir. She developed a passion for it from Chris Silva, her choir teacher at Judson Middle School in Salem. He had high expectations for quality and loved kids. Later, when Hayes went to Sprague High School, she was under the direction of Russ Christensen, who took the choir to two state titles while she was there. She continues to be involved with choir in her church. In high school, however, Hayes not only became skilled in singing, but learned to organize.

In 1995, when Hayes was a junior at Sprague, she was voted president of the choir. In that position, she did what a choir president would normally do: help with logistics, marshal kids on tours, meet with chaperones. But Hayes did something more: she organized a tour from scratch. The choir had gone to Disneyland her junior year, but the following year, no tour was planned. Christensen was happy to have the year off, but Hayes thought, This is my senior year, and our choir should go *somewhere*. It was too expensive to go to Disneyland again, but the choir could go to Seattle. Christensen said, "Fine, Cheyenne; if you want to go to Seattle, you make it happen."

Hayes needed to go to the initial parent meeting and convince mothers and fathers this was a great undertaking. The choir would raise most of the money with parents paying out of pocket no more than one hundred dollars. Hayes and her presidency would explain to them how the money would be raised: find fundraising companies, come up with ideas, submit those proposals to Christensen for review, and he either would veto or accept their methods for fundraising. Hayes went to companies that made chocolate bars or other items, found what percentage of money would go to the company, what percentage to the kids, the kids' level of commitment, how much product must be purchased up front and if terms were favorable, make a sales arrangement and receive a written agreement.

In Seattle, she would meet with chaperones to see if there were any unusual struggles with students. When the bus went to a location, she would be in charge of announcing the destination, such as going to Pacific Lutheran University, singing for the college program there and making sure the kids were respectful. She would have input on every place the choir would visit and why it was important. Christensen asked her opinion about fun places to visit such as Pike Place Market or the Seattle Center. He had Hayes sift through these details and report back to him. She needed a plan in words that made sense to the parents.

It was the first time Hayes faced a challenge on this scale, requiring effort, organization, passion and someone telling her if you want this bad enough, *go make it happen.*

She and the other members of her presidency convinced the parents and made it happen. The tour was successful. The experience made her more confident in her abilities.

This confidence translated to the future. When Cheyenne became engaged to Willie Hayes, they became franchisees of Izzy Pizza outlets in Olympia, Washington. That business gave Hayes ample experience in, as she puts it, "of organization and herding people." She also directed large-scale musicals at her church.

Not long after their marriage, Willie introduced Cheyenne to racquetball, and she started winning matches. Over time, she became the number one woman racquetball player in Washington State and the Pacific Northwest. She became part of the international pro tour of women, traveling to places like Cincinnati and Los Angeles to compete. She wanted to play the best in the world, but to do that, she would have to be gone for weeks at a time; she had young children at home and didn't want to do that. She decided that if she were not willing to meet players in the far reaches of the globe, maybe she could bring those players to her. She then considered something far more challenging than she had ever done before: she could start her own tournament in Olympia.

She had competed in other tournaments in her area and heard people talk about how a tournament should be run, what they liked and didn't like, and she developed her own understanding of what a proper tournament should be. One day she went to Bellingham near the Canadian border for a tournament and a light bulb went on. She came back and said to Willie, "We can do this. We can bring all those professional girls to us!"

Hayes found that she would need to raise $15,000 over nine months for a sport with which many people were not familiar. Racquetball, unlike tennis, was not considered lucrative. It was thought of—by a healthy minority at least—as a backwater, blue-collar sport. The first month or so it was "Crazy Cheyenne with a harebrained idea."

She started with small events: one-day shootouts and mini-tournaments where women paid $25 to compete. She raised money in other ways—bunco nights and similar events—but she also contacted business owners, some who played racquetball. To these owners already playing the sport, she explained what she wanted to do, that many people loved watching racquetball at the highest level. She got a few people on board with donations of $500 to $1,000 and she received money not only in cash but in kind. Costco, Fred Meyer, and other stores donated $50 to $100 gift cards to purchase breakfast food and Hayes worked the hotels to offer comp nights for players flying in. Other business owners starting noticing what was going on and as Hayes kept communicating, emailing, posting information, creating a buzz, people began to realize this was actually going to happen. Girls committed to fly in from Chile, Mexico, Canada, and elsewhere to compete, created more publicity.

Hayes hired a tournament staff of eight people, put a facility under contract and handled the accommodations and food for all the players. They did all the scheduling for matches at ten different courts with almost two hundred players going through winner and loser tournament brackets. Hayes put up $10,000 prize money for the pros with another $2,000 fun money spread out among the amateurs. She paid for a hotel room for the commissioner flying in from New York. She and her staff paid for promotional materials and put up a huge world map on the wall with photos of the players, a mini-bio for each and a string from the bio to the player's country of origin.

The first year, 2007, was the most difficult. Hayes created everything from the ground up, did all the documents herself and had to convince people that each challenge could be overcome. After the first year when so many people saw the expert level of play, as she and her staff were wrapping up, prior sponsors recommitted and new ones came forward.

Hayes ran the tournament for seven years: five years in Olympia and two in Seattle. Each year, she managed one large tournament and a second, smaller tournament focusing on local women players, especially women newly attracted to the sport.

Hayes has had several other opportunities since then, a large percentage of them associated with racquetball. She expects to accomplish something even if people around her don't think she can. She said, "People will say all the time, I'm going to run a tournament, but they don't realize how overwhelming it is and how much money it takes. I had to start early. I had to think through all the details and infuse passion with people around me, to buy into my vision. It meant remaining confident when people were not buying into it initially. Some people don't yet have that vision and need to see more evidence before they are on board. Sometimes you have to be alone for a while with your dream."

Cheyenne Hayes might have developed that dream no matter what, but her choir experience helped put her on that path.

Dick Withnell

"I don't have an ounce of music ability in me," Dick Withnell will tell you, "Not. One. Ounce." With those words, I knew he had to be in this book.

He wasn't totally truthful because he played trumpet in his father's band when he was in high school, but accepting the spirit of his statement, it is astounding how a man with so little musical talent can make such a mark on music.

Anyone living in Salem for long has heard of Dick Withnell. How could he not? For years he has had his Dodge dealership sitting on south Commercial Street in Salem with the large sign: WITHNELL MOTOR COMPANY. He purchased the dealership in 1980 when the prime rate was 23 percent and in five months, made it the number one Dodge dealer in Oregon. For twenty-two years, he ran the company, receiving quality awards from national publications such as *Time* and *Newsweek*. For many of those years, he was heavily involved with automobile dealer associations on state and national levels.

Withnell was not in Salem long before he supported civic activities in a major way. Particularly after he sold his dealership to his son, David, in 2002, he seemed to have his hands in every worthy cause imaginable: sentencing reform, better foster care, poverty reduction, family preservation, drug treatment programs. He was a noted philanthropist who supported his alma mater, Linfield College, The Boy Scouts of America, and several religious organizations.

Where does music fit in? Withnell could read music, but he didn't have the discipline to practice, didn't have the passion and was never going to be a musician, not even for an avocation. But he was affected by music at an early age. His father, Harold Withnell, was the band director at Astoria High School in extreme northwest Oregon for twelve years. In those days, the general feeling among some people was that only sissies were in the music programs. Withnell thought back to his father's teaching: "The program had athletes in it; it was held in high esteem. Kids played in the band who were not sissies. And it was all business: there were 175 kids in the concert bands and marching band." Withnell had been in the marching band. Harold was also the music supervisor, which gave him the power to hire and fire music personnel.

In addition to band instruments, Harold could play the organ, any mouthpiece instrument, just about anything. He was also a composer and Dick's mother had a natural singing voice—a beautiful soprano. Dick had a solid musical heritage from both parents.

Withnell naturally inherited a sympathy toward music education, but as he grew into adulthood, he focused on building his auto business and his overtures into civic affairs had nothing yet to do with music. But all along, Withnell knew something too many other people never learn: extracurricular activities keep many kids in school. He, himself, had not wanted to continue in high school, but sports kept him there. He knew, however, that he couldn't do the fun stuff unless he completed his academics. By staying in school, he and others understood that studying the essential subjects was necessary to go to college and get a job.

Withnell knew of a middle-school boy in Keizer who had a terrible home life living with a single parent. He was getting terrible grades but loved playing the trombone. Withnell said, "In the wisdom of the school, the administration put the boy in a study hall at the same period of the day he would be playing his trombone. The boy lasted another five days in school and now no one knows where he is." This story had a deep impact on Dick.

In the 1980s, through working on an initiative, Withnell got to know Bill Kendrick, the superintendent of Salem-Keizer at the time, and through Kendrick, the music supervisor, Karl Raschkes. What impressed Withnell about Raschkes was "his pursuit of excellence. He was the John Wooden of music; the John Wooden of the nation." This was important to Withnell, because he strove for excellence and coached his subordinates to do the same. Withnell was beginning to have influence on Raschkes and introduced him to an initiative called *Character Counts*, a program originating from Philadelphia, which adds to curriculum trustworthiness and other similar virtues. This program received considerable resistance from several people in Salem, but when Raschkes took it over, it rose in stature.

One evening, Withnell went to see *Mr. Holland's Opus*, a movie filmed in Portland, about a high achieving school band director. The movie deeply impressed Withnell, not just because it was filmed in Portland, not just because a fellow Portland auto dealer, Ron Tonkin, supplied the cars for the parade in the movie, or even because the parade marshal was an appliance dealer Withnell knew. *Mr. Holland's Opus* impressed Withnell because the band leader reminded him of his father. He went to Raschkes and came up with the idea of having kids in music watch the movie and based on that movie, write an essay. Top essays would be chosen, and Withnell would help the winners go to college. In 1996, the Harold J. Withnell Scholarship was born.

For the first two years, Withnell rented all the major movie theatres in Salem and had them show *Mr. Holland's Opus* to the Salem-Keizer music students. Raschkes obtained extra money from the district and, with Dick's support, bussed five hundred to six hundred kids to watch the movie. Students who had been recommended by Raschkes and their teachers and who participated in the All-City (all-star) band, orchestra, or choir were asked to write an essay on their impressions of *Mr. Holland's Opus*.

Raschkes went through the essays, and a student whose essay was chosen received a $1,000 scholarship. Raschkes pared the essays to eight or nine and sent them to Withnell to make the final cuts to three or four, but Withnell could never make the extra cuts. He and his wife read them and thought they were all good.

Withnell's scholarship program has been thriving for over twenty years. If a student wins a scholarship, he or she is invited to a luncheon at a nice restaurant along with his or her principal, music instructor and parents. A prominent person in town hands out the certificates, and the kids are invited to open the envelopes in which the scholarship and money is included.

In 2008, Withnell added a separate financial needs-based scholarship to provide music lessons—both instrumental and vocal—for middle-school and high-school students who demonstrate exceptional musical talent. Withnell believes strongly in keeping these vital extracurricular programs alive.

In about 2012, he was at a United Way function, sitting next to a girl who soon would become a high school senior. The girl was abundantly attired with tattoos and body piercings. He asked where she went to school.

"McKay."

"What are your interests?"

"Drama."

"How many kids are involved in drama?"

"Last year, we had 175 kids in drama, but this year, we will only have twenty-seven."

"Why?"

"They cut two teachers."

Withnell thought, *Can you imagine those 148 kids who aren't in drama now? If they were like her, do you think they would be in school?* Withnell stayed in school because he liked sports. Because he stayed in school, he is where he is now. He wants students to stay in school so they can turn their lives around and have the same opportunities.

Katie

I have never met Katie. I don't know her real name, and even if I did, I would have a difficult time finding her. If by a miracle I managed to track her down, a conversation with her could be awkward.

Katie was in Ben Stokes' middle-school band when he taught in California. One day, about six years after she graduated from middle school, (and apparently out of high school), Katie entered Stokes' band room at the end of a class period and walked up to him.

"Mr. Stokes, do you remember me?"

He did not recognize her. "I'm sorry, I don't."

When she said her name, he looked more closely and said, "Yes, I do remember you. In fact, I remember you well."

Katie appeared as if she was barely out of high school and, yet to Stokes, looked hardened beyond her years. They exchanged the typical pleasantries: Stokes referred to what she had done in class and what instrument she played. He asked her what she was doing now.

"Mr. Stokes, I just got out of rehab. The reason I made it through rehab is because of you."

Stokes was thinking, Oh, my goodness, seriously? This is huge!

"The confidence I got from playing in band helped me remember that I can get through this and quit doing drugs."

What startled Stokes the most was that he did not have a particularly close relationship with Katie. All teachers get to know certain students very well, but for Stokes, Katie was not one of them. She showed little promise with her instrument and almost never spoke to him. He recalled vaguely helping her position her fingers and get through the difficulties of learning her instrument. It did come back to Stokes that Katie stayed with the program, that she did not quit. But when she graduated, in his mind, that was the end of her. Until she reentered his band room six years later.

The Katie story is a classic example of progress in the classroom, we will never see in a performance on stage.

Juan Valdez

Some time ago, I traveled to Eugene to watch Juan Valdez perform a tuba recital. He would be accompanied on the piano by Dr. Lynn Kane, a faculty member at the University of Oregon. I didn't know what to expect. Tuba players aren't known for extended solos in bands and symphony orchestras.

As I walked into the music building on campus, a sizable group of people gathered outside Thelma Schnitzer Hall where the recital would take place. Most were friends, fellow players on the tuba or its smaller sibling, the euphonium. I sat in the second row, dead center where I could observe Valdez at close range, tapping buttons or moving slides on his Rube Goldberg-like device.

Everyone should go to a tuba recital at least once, especially if Valdez is behind the mouthpiece. He dazzled us with his rapid note successions and extraordinary range, all done by manipulating air through his lips. Valdez began *Capriccio* by Rodney Newton on a bass tuba and then switched to a contrabass for an arrangement of a concerto by Franz Joseph Haydn. He continued with his contrabass and switched back to the bass for the final number.

Like all wind instruments, the tuba is in a "family": you have the bass tuba and the contrabass but also the euphonium, which can be considered a "tenor tuba". Contrabass players can blow some of the lowest pitches in the musical world. I read that if all five valves are compressed, the tuba can make a C sound nearly an octave below the lowest note on a piano. The contrabass can also go surprisingly high. Valdez ended *The Effervescent Ballroom* on E above middle C and can play nearly an octave above that.

Just before the recital, Valdez took third place in the Northwest Regional Tuba Contest at Washington State University in Pullman, Washington—he had also been in a tuba-euphonium quartet that captured first place. He won the Oregon state high school tuba solo competition his senior year and received a full-ride scholarship to the University of Oregon. He was interviewed by the *Statesman Journal* in Salem and by KOIN television in Portland. The media people gravitated to Valdez not only because he excelled on the tuba but because he was a tuba player at all or a player of any substance. They discovered that Valdez was the product of two remarkable stories: the story of his parents and the story of himself.

JUAN VALDEZ WAS BORN IN ANAHEIM, CALIFORNIA, BUT HIS PARents were from Mexico. He traveled with them to Mexico to hear *banda* bands, much like mariachi bands but larger. The banda typically has ten trumpets, seven *superbones* (a trumpet/trombone hybrid, in essence a very large trombone), singers, woodwinds, and always a sousaphone in the background "ripping it" as Valdez remembered. Farther north in Mexico you will find a variation of the banda, *la banda nortena*, that includes a tuba, drum set, singers, and an accordion. Valdez grew up hearing this music and loved it.

Valdez's parents were not musical, but his maternal grandfather, Joel Matias, played clarinet in a banda in the *state* of Mexico, which borders Mexico City on three sides but is not a part of it. Not only did Joel play the clarinet, but he was the mayor of a town called St. Tomás. Being mayor was a prestigious position, almost like being a governor "if you do the right things," Valdez said. One of the perks was access to visas for his wife and children. When Joel's wife, Conchita came down with cancer; because Joel was in politics and had the financial means, his wife was brought to the United States for better care. Their daughter, Alma—Juan's mother—often flew with her own mother to California, staying for long stretches of time. In California, Alma went to school, picked up English, and over the course of time could be considered quite educated. Much later, when Alma moved to Salem, she intended to become a physician. Alma continued to stay in America, received a green card, which she renewed every five years. When Conchita passed away, Alma traveled back to Mexico to attend her funeral. On the return flight to California, her seat partner happened to be Juan Valdez's father (also named Juan Valdez). The two talked for the entire trip. Not long after, they married.

Juan Senior's background was vastly different from Alma's. He was poor, growing up on a small farm in southwest Mexico. Juan Senior was close to his own father, Martin Valdez, and loved to travel in the area with him. When Martin passed away, Juan Senior supported the family, mostly by raising cows on the farm, but there wasn't enough income and outside employment was scarce. Because Juan Senior was less close to his mother, Leonor Valdez, and not interested in attending school, in 1983, he made the decision to cross illegally into Texas looking for work.

To cross the border, Juan Senior needed to hire a coyote, who demanded $5,000 up front. Luckily Juan's family raised the money. The coyote knew all the routes and where immigration officers were stationed at any time. At twelve noon one day, the patrol cars went opposite ways for lunch. The coyote told Juan to move quickly. He made it into Texas successfully and it was now up to him to support his family back in Mexico.

Being in America did not initially make life easier for Juan Senior. For six months, he lived in a cardboard box under a tree. He had one blanket, and whatever money he could make was used for basic survival. Often he didn't have enough to eat. Juan Junior said, "He was a very skinny dude."

Despite everything, Juan Senior worked hard, traveling around the United States doing whatever he could. Juan Junior remembered that his father picked oranges in Florida.

Not only did Juan Senior work hard; he was resourceful and smart. He could get things done and could manage people. He was lucky that during the Reagan presidency, clemency was offered to illegal immigrants who had been in the United States for a certain time. Juan Senior was able to receive legal residence.

He linked up with the Oakley Corporation in southern California, which makes sunglasses and apparel. He started at the bottom and worked his way up. The leaders at Oakley were impressed with his talent and wanted to make him a vice president, but he didn't have a good enough command of English and was never offered the position. He and Alma were also becoming disenchanted with the gang culture that permeated the area where they lived. They did not want to see their only child, Juan, become a part of that. They decided to move out, and Oregon offered opportunity. Juan Senior became a manager of Mallory's Dairy outside Silverton, and Alma worked at Kinko's (now FedEx) in south Salem. The money wasn't great, but Juan's parents had always been a unit of one; all money went into a joint account. They worked together to make ends meet.

Juan Junior found himself attending school at Yoshikai Elementary in northeast Salem. In the fourth grade, he joined a string orchestra class and became attracted to the cello. He had seen Yo-Yo Ma on YouTube and thought "he was super cool; his facial expressions were amazing." He decided to give the cello a try. He didn't know if he was one of the better cello players, but the emotional aspect of music, the feeling in his fingertips, having this facial expression; he knew he had some kind of musical voice in him. Whatever instrument he touched—the piano, the trumpet, the cello—he wondered why he was feeling like this. Why was playing giving him this essence? He felt this in general music at Yoshikai, singing in church and playing the recorder; he always had this urge. Playing the recorder was standard in elementary school; he picked it up quickly and the fingering was easy. He liked the pitch, the melody. He always had music in his life.

When Valdez entered the fifth grade, he and his parents went to a concert where there were trumpets and all the other brass instruments. Valdez heard the trumpets, the high notes, the low notes, and how beautiful it was. His mother told him he should play the trumpet, and he enthusiastically agreed. He liked how the trumpet player could play high, squint his eyes, puff his cheeks, and turn red. His parents didn't push him to play the trumpet; it was mostly his own decision.

In fifth grade, he was being taught by Jaimie Hall, considered by many to be the best pre-high school band teacher in Salem. Hall would strive to build a relationship with each student from the beginning. This was hard when he might have more than sixty kids in a class, half of them dropping out in the first three months. Valdez ended up having Hall for a teacher in fifth grade, for three years in middle school, and for four years in the high school jazz band.

That was all in the future. In the fifth grade Valdez stayed with the trumpet, but when he transferred to Adams Stephens Middle School for sixth grade, there was a change in his schedule. He had always been bilingual, but for some reason, he struggled to comprehend the information he was reading in English. He needed to take an additional class to reinforce his English skills. He expected to be in the intermediate band, but this additional reading class was scheduled against the intermediate time slot, and the only other choice was to take beginning band. This was deflating, particularly when several of his sixth grade peers were already in the advanced band, the top band in middle school.

Valdez went to see Jaimie Hall. They went to the counselor's office, looked at his schedule, and decided that it would be best for Valdez to be in beginner's band. Juan was not thrilled, but Jaimie told him that the next year he would lose two tuba players, and if he had no tubas, he would essentially have no band. By this time, Valdez had his first concert in the beginning band playing trumpet, but his mother had heard the advanced band and told Juan that she wanted him to be in that band someday. Hall told Valdez that if he would play tuba in the beginning band for the remainder of the year, the next year he would be in advanced band. Valdez said,

"Jaimie must have sensed something. I had always been a big guy, bigger than my classmates, and Jaimie might have taken note of my physical characteristics."

Valdez found playing the tuba to be easy, because the mouthpiece was bigger. He played by blowing into a downstream angle; he was more suited to that. As he looked back, he said he was "not all that great" on the trumpet, but he had that passion for music, and his embouchure was more suited to the tuba. Hall told Valdez that from the beginning, he had a big sound filling up a room, not a tight sound choking him but a sound that resonated. For Valdez, it had always been "sound, sound, sound"; he wanted to have that big sound that kept getting bigger.

With the tuba, he had to start with the beginning band, but it was fun. He could fill the room, and being at the "bottom" of the band was "really cool." It took off from there. In seventh and eighth grade, there were three tubas in the top band. Juan was second tuba, but he kept improving.

Meanwhile, his parents had their struggles through the years. One day, in 2006, a heavy snow year when Valdez was still in elementary school, his father was driving a truck out of Mallory's Dairy. He got out of the truck for some reason and put on the emergency brake, but the truck was parked on a hill and started rolling down toward oncoming traffic. Juan Senior ran to open the door and turn the truck to avoid traffic—which he was able to do—but he slipped on the ice. His hand hit the ground hard and he broke a bone in eight places. He was out of work for a year because he had to have three surgeries on his hand. When Juan Junior was in sixth grade, his father suffered another injury at the dairy, falling on a post that penetrated into his upper thigh. This time, he was hospitalized for five months.

Alma was forced to support the family. On her modest salary at Kinko's, she paid the regular bills and all medical bills. At the same time, gas prices were sky high, creating more burden for Alma—already strapped for money—driving across town for work. When Juan Senior was working, she fortunately saved much of his earnings, which she used to stay current on bills.

When Juan Junior was in the eighth grade, his mother's papers expired and she was unable to renew them. Now she was technically illegally in the United States. She was not going to be forced to move to Mexico, but after Juan Senior's second injury, the government put him on disability. Juan Valdez Senior was not the type of person who was going to sit at home. As Juan Junior put it, "He was going to go out and work because he had been working since he was three years old. He was a workaholic." His parents talked it over and decided to move back to Mexico, to St. Tomás, the homeland of her parents. They were starting from the beginning, but the local people knew Juan Senior had good character and because he had shown talent in a managerial position, he was appointed by the city to be a judge. His mother opened a small convenience store and they have become well established in Mexico.

Juan Junior did not want to move back to Mexico. There was little music education to speak of in Mexican schools, certainly not where he was going. If he moved down there, it would be like dropping off a cliff. His parents gave him the option of staying or going. In seventh grade, he began to learn more about himself. He had struggled trying to fit in with the popular kids, students who didn't care about anything and were out to have fun. But he was also part of the band and was living the band life, being with kids who played music. He was going through a thought process and felt "two-faced." Sometimes he ate lunch in the cafeteria, sometimes in the band room. By eighth grade, he was taking band more seriously.

Despite not wanting to leave Salem, Valdez was still in terrible conflict about parting with his parents. He confided his feelings with Hall, but it took some time for him to make up his mind whether to go with his parents or stay in Salem. In seventh grade,

Valdez met Daniel Hendrick, who had transferred from Houck Middle School to be in Hall's music program. Hendrick had gone back and forth to being a first or second trumpet and was a "really nice guy," Valdez said. Valdez talked to Hendrick, who said that Valdez could move in with him and his family. Hendrick's family lived in the Houck area, which meant that when Valdez and Hendrick graduated from middle school, they would be going to North High School. At the same time, Jaimie Hall was being moved to the newly opened Straub Middle School in West Salem and would be teaching jazz band at West High. Valdez and Hendrick knew about the great program at West under Todd Zimbelman.

While still in eighth grade, both boys auditioned to be in the Wind Ensemble, the top band at West High. To transfer to West, they had to be in a class not offered at North High. They both chose German. Valdez had to take German for two years. (today, he can count and say "around the corner" in German.)

Hendrick made it into the Wind Ensemble, but Valdez did not. There was one opening for a trumpet player but none for tubas. Zimbelman already had two tuba players in his top group and didn't need any more. He believed in having only one instrument to a part, as a college band should have. When All-City (an annual event in Salem featuring an all-star high-school band, orchestra, and choir) loomed in late February, the top players of every instrument were encouraged to audition to be part of the all-star band. It was January, audition time for All-City. The best tuba players in Salem competed including the two tuba players in Zimbelman's Wind Ensemble. They auditioned behind a curtain so the judges could only hear them and their decision would not be influenced by seeing someone they knew and liked. At the end of the tuba audition, Valdez was judged to be the number one tuba player in Salem-Keizer, higher than the two current tuba players in the West High Wind Ensemble. For a freshman to take first place in any All-City audition was unheard of. When Zimbelman found out about it, even though he was at capacity with tubas in his top band, he told Valdez that he had no choice but to put him in his group.

To work in Zimbelman's band was to embark on a steep learning curve. Valdez said,

> Every six weeks, he would throw new music at us. His philosophy was to have us experience different styles, textures and colors; skills we could implement into our repertoire. Most band directors just say play in tune, but Mr. Zimbelman had us tune our instruments to a tuning device to makes sure all of our frequencies matched to be absolutely in tune with each other. He wanted us to play every single note on our horns and figure what we needed to do to adjust to the other players. We did extensive singing with solfège; part of his pedagogy was singing, so we could more easily hear the correct pitch. He would have us sing the music before we played it. We would do that every day. We did sight-reading once a week. Or he would do something even more ambitious: he would have us prepare and play a piece we would never perform. That was the preparation and mindset we needed. We were constantly faced with new music, having a great product. He always said, "If you are going to do something, you have to do it well.

Juan Valdez Jr. has a full ride at the University of Oregon and plans on going to graduate school. He thinks that his band professor, Dr. Dorsey, is amazing. He says the only difference between the band at West High and the same at the University of Oregon is that the university has better overall talent. Valdez is the only tuba player in the university symphony orchestra.

His goal is to play in a professional symphony orchestra. The competition for any top symphony position is fierce. People audition from all over the world. When I spoke with him, there was an opening in the Seattle Symphony, and he plans to go there and audition. He says that even if he does not get the position, it will be good preparation. Every position of any worth requires an audition. Each audition is another step, which will prepare Valdez for the day when he does the *real* gig.

Julie Rundquist

Julie Rundquist always puts family first. She taught kindergarten in northeast Salem for twelve years to be able to spend more time with her children when they were still at home. Otherwise, I don't know of anyone more enveloped, often imbued by music. She played violin for the Salem Chamber Orchestra for twenty-six years before it folded, and she was with the Salem Symphony before that too shut down. She said,

> I am in the middle of this amazing sound that everyone is creating. Just the feeling I am able to have, the emotion, the sound, the tone colors; I can't get that anywhere else. Piano is fun and beautiful (she is accomplished on that instrument also), but I am by myself. To accompany is still with only one other person, but to be in a symphony, that is the ultimate.

Rundquist has been musically encompassed in another profound way. Her father, Keith Reed, played the cornet and trumpet; her mother, Margaret Reed, played the violin. Julie, her father, and her daughter Lindsay, on the violin, have all participated with the All-Northwest orchestra in Bellevue, Washington. Her son, Peter, plays the French horn and is a music teacher in Keizer and her husband, Phil, taught band (an amazing program, she said) at Walker Middle School in West Salem for twenty-five years. Familywise, music doesn't get much more complete than that.

For the past six years, Rundquist has taught string instruments full time at Crossler Middle School in south Salem. Not long before we met, she took her top orchestra to a festival at Mt. Hood Community College east of Portland and received the highest rating. I watched her string groups play in a concert at Crossler in the spring of 2017 and was amazed at the stair-step difference in skill level: from elementary school strings, to beginners in middle school and intermediates, and finally the polished performance of Rundquist's advanced string orchestra.

Growing up in Boise, Idaho, Rundquist desired to be a teacher at an early age. She and her little brothers would go into the basement where she would "teach them school"; in her own words, she was "bossy," but she was in her element. And from the beginning, she loved music. She was drawn to choir and orchestra, although she acknowledged that she found the violin more challenging. She worked hard, always trying to improve and gain the skills necessary to be proficient when she entered high school. In junior high, she passed an audition to be in the All-City group. In high school, she remained in choir and orchestra but also played in the Boise Treasure Valley Youth Symphony the year it was established. In 1977, she auditioned for the Boise Philharmonic (the professional symphony in Boise) and was accepted into that as well. The folks at the Philharmonic would not allow her to play unless she remained in the youth symphony, so in her later years in high school, she was in high school choir and orchestra, the Treasure Valley Youth Symphony, and the Boise Philharmonic.

When Rundquist played for the Philharmonic, she was in select student company. Five or six players from high schools around Boise were there: one bass player became a public school teacher, another still plays for the Philharmonic, another plays chamber music in Boston; all of them are still active players.

If Rundquist rose in prominence with her playing skills, she had the good fortune to acquire increasingly good instruments. She had played on a "clunker" in fifth grade and when she entered sixth grade, her parents paid for a violin that was "a step up but nothing special." When she started taking private lessons, her teacher told her that she needed a better violin, but her parents didn't want to pay for another violin. Meantime, Mary Boyd, an older woman who sat next to Rundquist in the Philharmonic, told her she was going to sell one of her high-quality violins and Julie could purchase it if she wanted. Rundquist bought the violin, using every penny she made from summer jobs and from the Philharmonic, paying $840 over three years, which was no small amount in 1977.

Several years later, Boyd came down with dementia, which meant she needed someone at home to care for her. Her husband, a lawyer in town, asked Julie, when she came home from college for the summer, if she would like to be Mary's aid and Julie agreed. She had Mary's friends over for lunch, took Mary places, brought Mary with her to violin lessons, and generally, Julie said, they had a wonderful time together. Mary's husband wanted Julie to stay, but she needed to go back to college and found someone to stay with Mary during the school year. When Julie came back the following summer, Mary's condition worsened enough that it was imperative she be in a nursing home. By happenstance Rundquist signed up to work at the home and was assigned to Mary's unit. She continued to care for Mary, and when Mary passed away a year later, her husband gave Julie Mary's other violin. It was a French violin of high quality, the type used by players in professional symphony orchestras. It was something Julie said she could never have paid for herself.

During Rundquist's high school years, she went to summer music camps. One in Sun Valley provided her a scholarship to attend the University of Missouri in Columbia. Rundquist loved Missouri; it was not top of the line but was the right school to teach string pedagogy, the methods to teach strings. Rundquist had good training at Missouri; all the celebrated concert groups coming through Kansas City and St. Louis stopped in Columbia. Rundquist said the music department was "big enough for great things to happen and yet small enough to give tremendous help." She completed a five-year program in four years. She says, "I was taking twenty-two to twenty-four credits at a time. I did not go there in the summers but took several classes at Boise State, sixteen credits in all to make it work." She graduated from the University of Missouri in 1982.

As much as Rundquist enjoyed being in Columbia, she was a westerner and wanted to return to Boise. She couldn't find a job in Boise and settled for a first job in Marshall, Missouri, a town with a population of twelve thousand, sixty miles west of Columbia (interestingly enough, her grandfather had grown up there). Like most people from a larger city who teach in a small town, she liked the people but found the music program lacking. She thought she made a difference teaching strings; she took her orchestra to a festival in Sedalia and the kids were excited just to be there. The performance quality for a high school orchestra in Marshall was significantly lower than her middle school orchestra at Crossler. Still, she was excited that she had made progress in a school that did not have a strong program.

If Rundquist just taught strings at Marshall, that would have been one thing, but she taught all music: elementary, middle school, high school, all choirs, all bands. She was taking on too much and faced problems with managing the kids. Some teachers learn it easily, Rundquist said, but she did not. She found the kids' behavior hard to understand, and she is still in the process of sorting that out. She said, "It is something you have to learn no matter where you go, something you gain with experience. You don't just enter with total command in a classroom environment." The experience in Marshall was stressful for her.

At the end of the year, one of the other teachers suggested Rundquist should go into violin performance. She made up her mind she would do just that: go back to the University of Missouri and get a degree. She set up a fellowship with the university and had no intention of teaching again.

Life intervened. She traveled back to Boise for the summer and met her future husband, Phil. She met him briefly when she came home the previous Christmas; he was teaching band in nearby Meridian. Rundquist went back to Missouri, packed her belongings, and moved back to Boise to marry Phil, but with no immediate job prospects. She found jobs teaching general music part time in elementary schools and directing a high school orchestra along with twenty-six private violin and piano students. She taught six years in Boise, but her jobs were general music at the elementary level with only one or two classes of strings instruction. She wanted a full-time job teaching orchestra, but the Boise District never had any openings.

In 1989, Karl Raschkes entered the picture. He was a judge at a festival in Idaho and watched her orchestra. Rundquist was on maternity leave at the time and was not at the festival to greet Raschkes. Later, he called Julie and Phil and wanted them to come to Salem. Boise had a great music program, but it was a no-brainer for them to move. The salary would double for Phil and be one and a half times more for Julie. They could both teach in their chosen fields, but still it was hard emotionally to move. Both of their families were in the Boise area.

When Rundquist came to Salem, it was with the promise that she would teach half time so that she could spend more time with her child. She did teach half time but was forced to travel to nine different schools. After she gave birth to her second child, she went back to school to get her masters in elementary education. She taught kindergarten for twelve years, first grade for one year and fourth grade for one year.

During those years, Raschkes found her again and asked, "When are you going to come back and teach strings?" He kept after her, and she kept saying no, but when her son was out of school, she said yes. She was a temp at Whiteaker, and the next year Raschkes hired her at Crossler full time. In addition to teaching at Crossler, she teaches elementary strings at Liberty and Schirle in South Salem. Career-wise, she has finally found a home.

Jim Taylor

When I met with Jim Taylor in March 2017, he was no longer teaching choir at McNary High School. I found him at Claggett Creek Middle School teaching drama, audio/video production, and just about everything related to food, all approached with his trademark zeal.

In recording arts, his main activity is producing a news broadcast. The day begins with a YouTube of the broadcast shown to members of the faculty and others. It shows one kid at a desk reading the news, teleprompter at hand so he can read into the camera. Following that, other kids write a script for the next day's news with Taylor's help. Then the kids all walk into the next room to shoot the next day's news: one student directs, others are on backdrop with lights, cameras, and teleprompters in place. Another student inputs this into a computer. The day drifts by until sixth period when three kids run in to begin editing the YouTube on the computer and, when finished, email the total product, which will be shown the next morning. This news is about the school and can cover all manner of subjects; a day's broadcast watched by staff could be on the environment. The kids do everything: film, write scripts, edit, add music, do design and graphic work, provide words, riddles and bloopers for the day, and anchor. The recording arts class is so popular that some drama programs had to be cancelled to accommodate for it.

Then Taylor makes his wild switch to food. The students do everything you can imagine: cooking, dehydration, storage, recipe design. Taylor told me people with low incomes (many whose kids attend Claggett Creek) waste the most food. He said,

> For the money spent, we know from studies that people of low income go to fast-food restaurants and don't go grocery shopping. So we take a starch, a protein, vegetables, and I show them how to take ten dollars and turn it into four to five meals for four or five people. We show them the economic and nutritional value of eggs and the ability to turn eggs into fifty different products. We do the math for affordability and efficiency. We teach them how to dehydrate, make jams and jellies and their own chicken stock, almost the homesteader kind of thing.

His big dream is for the school to have its own vegetable garden.

Taylor only knows only one gear: overdrive. When he was at McNary, he was teaching ninety to one hundred hours a week. That was why he finally had to bail out and do something different, but he said, "This is who I am. I am the nutty professor; I just want to teach all the time." He comes by his freneticism naturally.

> I would tell the kids who are making biscuits, Grandma would rattle pots and pans so everyone would get out of bed to help make biscuits and cinnamon rolls. At twelve years old, that was what I was doing at 6:30 a.m. At 10:00 a.m., I was out chopping wood with my grandfather. At noon, I made lunch. At 1:30, I was out with Grandpa doing woodworking in his shop. At 3:30, I was knitting and crocheting with Grandma. At 5:00 p.m., we would be out gardening, so I grew up in this world where we were doing all these things all the time. We didn't go out to restaurants; we all cooked. My night was Tuesday night; I was responsible for everything. I had to do the cooking and cleaning. It was something we were brought up to do, be independent and be responsible for the people around us.

He never slowed down at McNary. For the ten years he was there (fall of 2005 through spring of 2016), he had at one time the largest music program in the state of Oregon: five hundred students on the roster including his students in guitar. All the time he was there, his *low* was 325 kids in choir alone. One year, he had 135 students in his Concert Choir.

The same year he had his huge Concert Choir, he founded the Highlander Classics, which had a high of seventy kids. He had an eight-piece string group accompany the Highlander Classics, and he took them to state. One year, he had the concert choir *and* the Highlander Classics in the state competition at the same time. It threw the organizers into a tizzy; they had to come up with new rules for district and state. OSAA (Oregon School Activities Association) had to change the rules again because he had the Highlander Classics with all the instruments. Other schools started doing the same, and it was beginning to get out of hand. For several years, he was enormously successful at state. In 2010 and 2012, his Concert Choir came in second. In 2011, McNary was first.

The activity didn't stop with his big choirs. The last year he was at McNary, his kids in various configurations performed a total of sixty-eight concerts! Most of the burden fell on smaller groups. He said,

> We did a lot of micro concerts. We would do half-hour to forty-five-minute concerts at Rotary, or we would take twenty kids to a retirement center for a one to one-and-a-half-hour performance. The kids would do Christmas caroling—this wouldn't even count as a concert—and sing at fifty different places in seven days. People would walk through the door and sit down to listen to us in the choir room or the theatre or we were at major luncheons, district or state events, at Willamette University for a choral leader workshop, the same at Oregon State University and Portland State University. They just added up, added up. With all the jazz groups, artists, and so forth, it is nothing for this school district to have two weekends of festivals a month, so in nine months there were eighteen festivals just like that. That was eighteen weekends of work. At McNary, we would do at least five full-fledged concerts with all the choirs on stage. And of course there were the tours where we would perform seven concerts in three days.

If this weren't enough, during the second half of his last year when the orchestra teacher was fired, Taylor stepped in and taught the orchestra class. He said, "That was one of the highlights of my career. It was thrilling." But when he applied to be the permanent orchestra teacher, he was turned down; he didn't have the background for it. He said, "I did this by burning myself out, and that is why I am now out of music and teaching at Claggett Creek."

The sound of Taylor's choirs was not like most of the other choirs in the district whose directors aimed for the northern Lutheran sound with little vibrato. Andy Thomas, choir director at Whiteaker Middle School, described the McNary choir sound as "very big, very mature, very loud and inspired. His choirs were more like the choirs of Chuck Graber." Taylor said,

> My choirs didn't sound like David Brown's or Will McLean's. Mine were more like Kerry Burtis when he was at North—big, open, and robust. I like the kids to be open with their voices. Every year it is different because I have different kids but I am not about the perfect unified vowel. I want the kids to learn about their voices.

Andy Thomas said, "Jim student-taught with Graber and picked up a lot of Graberisms. Of anyone in choir, he reminds me the most of Graber. He is not into competitions." Taylor said,

> I think I was there to serve the student, to create opportunity. I never thought of myself as a choir teacher but a music teacher, an arts teacher. My philosophical bent comes from Gary Frame, my high school teacher at Sprague. He wanted to teach the student, not work for the trophy. Some just want to teach their craft. Gary influenced me as much as anyone. Gary has compassion, empathy, sincerity; I knew he was a religious man, and it showed in that humble servitude.

Two other teachers who influenced Taylor were Edwin Snyder at Western Oregon University and Maurice Skones at the University of Arizona.

> Snyder was much more the Viking, the gladiator. He would push you into the arena. Skones was in his head, it was all intellectual. Gary Frame was about the heart, Snyder about the brawn, and

Skones about the intellect, so I got all three legs of the stool. And then there was Graber, that big old engine in the back of the thing.

Like Graber, Taylor follows his own drummer. Most high schools in Salem-Keizer (and elsewhere in Oregon) stick to the three main disciplines (choir, orchestra and band), but Taylor believes that the population at large includes multifaceted musicians. Being stuck in a category bothers him.

We have an administration that says teach our kids for college and career. My opinion is that if the district wants to build a larger profiled student, then let us reach to all kids on the outside who need music in their lives. What if a kid in college is so depressed and doesn't know what to do but knows how to pick up a guitar and sing a song? I have my guitar or piano to get me through. I didn't have to be in choir, marching band, or sectionals.

Taylor believes a strong curriculum matters, but more importantly, the passion of the teacher matters.

Passion in the classroom translates to kids showing up for class, finishing school, finding a path in middle school that is going to guide them through high school. I want to create opportunities for these other kids to perform if they want to. They could perform in class, or even better, cabaret events, coffee houses or concerts. I worked hard to make more music opportunities. We know kids are happier with music. We know it makes better, stronger, smarter kids. If they are that, they will graduate, and that is all we are concerned about. In Oregon, 75 percent of all students graduate, which is below the national average, but in my program, three kids in ten years did not graduate. I could name their names. In ten years, I probably taught close to three thousand students hands-on in my classroom. Kids in music follow through.

Taylor's view of outsiders inspired him to start the guitar program.

I was looking at that gap of kids who weren't doing anything. I remembered watching this kid walk down the hall carrying a guitar on his back; he would sit out at lunchtime and just whittle away on his guitar. I walked up and talked to him and asked what he was doing. He said, "I just like to play." I asked, "How would you like to play in my jazz group?" He played with the jazz group, and all of a sudden three or four other kids I had never met were showing up for concerts. They were friends of the guitar player. I asked them, "Why don't you come play for me?" With that, I had a studio production class, forty-plus kids: seven guitar players, four drummers, four bass players, fifteen singers doing a capella singing, a rock-and-roll band, a ukulele group and they would all meet at the same time. I would break them out into seven, eight, or nine different groups, and this was my class. They along with audio and recording engineers, were down in the studio, the first period every day, making music all the time, two concerts every month.

They let me start this class because I was bringing new kids into the program. The principal let me do this. Justin Lieuallen, the vice principal at McNary, and I were talking one day. He said a guitar class would be awesome, and I agreed. We had someone who was a part-time assistant who was doing theory and piano teaching and we found we could fit in one more class, so I said, "Let's start a guitar class." By November before Thanksgiving break in 2015, I went to Uptown Music and said to Paul Elliot, "Paul, I have an idea, let's start a Play it Forward—he came up with that name—donation program. We advertised like mad through all his emails, all of Uptown's contacts, and asked for people to donate five guitars to McNary High School, and Uptown will donate one brand new high-quality guitar. We ended up with forty guitars in six weeks. We started the class in January of 2016. It is still active and going. Paul and I put all those guitars up on the wall.

I also did piano labs. It started with Jeff Kuhns, who is the captain of Keizer police, a student of my father at McKay and whose son was in my program at McNary. He and I were talking—our choir kids had done some Rotary events—and Jeff asked me, "What would really help your program grow?" I immediately thought back to a piano class I had with Gary Frame who had keyboards on a rickety old cafeteria table. We would all sit at these tiny little keyboards and practice. The keyboard case would open, and we would close them all after we were finished and put them

> in the corner until the next day. I said it would be great to offer a piano class, because kids who want to be successful in a performance or education in college need piano and theory classes. Jeff asked how much a piano lab would cost. I asked Paul at Uptown, and he figured the amount could be as low as $16,000 for twelve keyboards. Paul went to Roland Company, they gave us a discount, Paul donated some money, my families and groups raised money, Rotary matched it, and we got our twelve keyboards for $16,000. We bought six and Rotary bought six. We got the lab. The smart thing is that we bought high-quality equipment and it all still works. The keyboards have been at McNary for six or seven years now. There is still a piano lab, the keyboards get used a lot, and there are still people teaching it.

Taylor's view of all-inclusivity extended to raising money. When he first came, the choir had a once-a-year event that made approximately $20,000, but Taylor would sit at lunch with the majority of the art teachers, photo art, and so forth and they would complain about not getting enough funding. He said,

> The football program at University of Oregon funds all the other sports; why couldn't choir be the football of arts? We grouped together to share profits and called the evening Knight of Arts, combining all fine arts together, including theatre, graphic design, studio art and multimedia. The cool thing was that everyone could be involved: the graphic design group would make ads, studio art offered art for auction; there was a theatrical show and musical events. The booster group now includes all the arts on paper; we set it up that way. All art groups can participate if they wish. Maybe fifteen to twenty people were on the whole committee, one each from each art, but we had tons of people helping with Knight of Arts. The other purpose of the fundraiser was to start a scholarship fund. Last year we made $48,000 from the Knight of Arts. It included every art program, a live auction, silent auction, art show, theatrical show, and musical performances.

At first, Taylor had no intention of doing anything like Knight of Arts at McNary.

The Knight of Arts came to us through Matt Swenson, whom I met and is the choir director at Boise High School. I was in Boise and got invited to his big madrigal event they do at Christmas. I thought that was amazing; they were pulling in ten to twelve thousand dollars a night by having a big feast. They had tables, wenches, the whole mystique. He had a hundred costumes built up over fifty years. We became fast friends and he said, "Borrow my costumes, put them in a U-Haul, take them to Salem, use them, clean them and bring them back." For six years, I would fly over on a weekend, drive the costumes back to Salem, we would use them and three months later, I would drive them back, and each time, I would do a little workshop with his kids. It was great and that is how it started: borrowing from a friend, then taking it a step further and including orchestra and band, but my lunchtime visits with the other arts people expanded all of that. At lunchtime, the idea of hearing my colleagues and realizing that choir could be the football team of the arts. They have benefitted from that.

Another part of Taylor's legacy was giving high school students important responsibilities.

When I first came, I was able to hire an office manager, who came in and worked for up to two years getting things organized, including the library organized and dealing with the massive influx of kids. She was creating systems so we could function better, but that work got transferred over to students who were able to do it. I created a program of student office managers who did exceptional work. Some kids acquired great skill sets out of that. They planned the tours, two to Ashland and one to Seattle. They didn't do New York or Disneyland—I was slightly sane. It was a plan they could manage and they could work with repeat information going to the same places. By my third year, it was the kids who were running it."

"I came up with that idea because my dad was in business; he would talk about how to integrate with other departments in the building. I inherited that mind-set to try to integrate with other people. I reached out to the business classes and found kids who were interested in business, management, and marketing in college and had them come in and work in that capacity. They weren't choir kids doing it but kids from business/marketing coming in and doing this for the choir kids. It was an opportunity for kids to practice the skill set they were going to use in their careers. There were some who would leave choir after their sophomore year and do that. If kids were in the office, they were not in choir. They did office work. If you came into my classroom, 130 kids were there singing, but in my office, there would be three to five kids working on the business of the choir. They did not sing. They ran it. We had weekly meetings and we would make a game plan for the week. We would set up expectations, protocols, and they wrote the emails. I would read them and approve them. They wrote the letters, planned the tours, made the phone calls; they would do all the legwork and then I would send an email to lock this in. One, Jason Trinh, who is now running his family's restaurants, was a great kid. Nicole Elwell is moving to Africa to do a nursing outreach program there. Jennifer Lewis started in choir but went into business. Nicole was one of my first business kids. Her sister, Lindsey, became the manager after that. When I was in high school, I was in the choir with their mother, Julie Smith. It was neat to have her kids in my program. It was fun because there was great continuity. They could share information and were friends with each other. Every year, there was always one office manager, one lead student. Nicole was one, Lindsey was one, Jennifer was one, Jason was one. There were some really top-notch kids.

When we got the piano lab, Lindsey, who is a fantastic pianist, started doing after-school piano lessons for kids at risk and low-income kids. We ran hundreds of kids from our elementary feeder schools through the after-school program in the back of the choir room. Many of those kids became choir kids or music kids as they came to high school. Lindsey worked with Katy Flanigan; the two of them ran the piano program. For two years, literally hundreds of kids came through this program they offered after school. That was part of the deal with Rotary: give something back to the community. We came up with that concept, and it worked beautifully. I even had kids helping me teach piano who had been elementary kids learning from Katy and Lindsey five years earlier.

IF TAYLOR IS A VISIONARY, HE CREDITS MUCH OF THAT TO HIS unusual background. No one could come from a more education-based background than Jim Taylor. He has grandparents who taught, great aunts and uncles who taught, and some who still teach. Both siblings were teachers along with several cousins.

> We always made the joke that a family reunion was a faculty meeting. Everyone was in education in one shape or form. I was always around these teachers who never talked about bad kids, because the kids were engaged. They cared about the kids and kept the kids busy. If kids are busy, they can't get into trouble; that is why music and electives are such a great outlet.

Taylor's mother and father were teachers. His dad worked at Sprague and McKay, and his mom worked at McKinley, Walker, and Judson. His dad was in business, math, and driver's education and was a basketball coach. His mom was in special ed.

> The last part of her career, she became an administrative assistant, because the special ed work was harrowing. She worked with low-functioning children with broken bones and control issues the kids created. She finished working with kids at risk at Judson, but both my parents were stellar teachers. I have uncles and aunts in teaching all over the place. My sister is a teacher at a Catholic School in Woodburn, but she started in the Salem-Keizer School District. She is a second grade teacher this year, but has done preschool through sixth grade. I have a brother who taught at Indiana University for a while. Now he is a brewmeister in Portland. He went from German linguistics and philosophy to brewing German beer.

If Taylor had an uber background imbedded in education, the music part of that education came early. He had great music in preschool and kindergarten; music was big with his father's mom, Grandma Taylor, and it was important with the Kings, his mom's parents.

We were listening to it, playing it. Grandma Taylor, who lived in California, was always playing the piano. I sat on her lap as she played. We sang all the time in the car. We were never not making music in some way. Mom and Dad were not musicians, but they loved to sing, to make music as singers, but there was nothing professional about their musical experience. There were pictures of me in diapers singing, grabbing something and pretending it was a microphone, putting headphones on and singing Frank Sinatra. I was three years old. I tell the kids all the time, "You can be in the seventh grade and know what you want to do." Between my seventh and eighth grade year in the summer, we went to church, and the priest gave a sermon on avocations: what are you going to be when you grow up? Mom took the cue and asked all of us as we were driving home, "What do you want to be when you grow up?" I said, "I want to be a choir director." I think there was some tension with them thinking about another educator in the family. They didn't say no, but they didn't really want me to be a teacher. I did hear from Dad now and then suggesting that I should put all that talent and energy into something that will make more money, because we always scraped for money.

I had a good elementary teacher and a phenomenal middle school teacher, Debra Klatz, and then Gary Frame at Sprague. With Debra Klatz and Gary Frame, I was bound to do music. On the drive home, Mom asked,

"If you are going to teach choir, what will you have to do?"

I said, "I'm going to sing in choir."

"Mom said, "That is not going to be enough. Think about these other kids, kids all over the country who want to be choir directors—what are they doing?"

"I don't know."

"Well, find out."

I talked to my teachers. They said, "You have to know how to play the piano," so I started taking piano lessons. They said, "Not only do you need to sing well, but you need to know how to sing, what the mechanics are," so I started taking voice lessons. Then I asked for every opportunity I could get to do more at school. I jumped into everything.

In college, I expanded by playing the bassoon in band. With the bassoon, I went from lessons to first chair in eighteen weeks; I was determined. I went to Western Oregon University, was there with Myra Brand. She was phenomenal. When I walked in there, Myra said, "Be the best singer you can be. Let's think of you as a professional singer." I had Edwin Snyder, who did extraordinary things. He was at First Methodist Church for many years as the local Sunday director, an extraordinary conductor. He was the choral director at WOU. I had a fabulous education with him. He told me to be the best conductor and educator I can be. They pushed me in all three areas: Snyder just pushed and pushed me as a conductor, Brand as a singer, and both of them pushed me as an educator. You know how to sing now, teach someone to sing. You know how to conduct, now conduct, and so I worked my tail off. During my freshman year, Snyder said, "You need to go and start teaching now, because in four years when we put you out as a student teacher and you don't like working with kids, you will have lost four years of training.

They did not have practicums then, so I asked, "What do I do?" Snyder said, "Go down to Central High School (in Monmouth), and ask Russ Christensen if you can volunteer in his classroom." Russ had been at Central for ten years, so I knocked on his door.

"I'm Jim Taylor. I would like to volunteer for you."

"What do you know how to do?"

"I'm really big into jazz, musical theatre, and choir."

"See you tomorrow morning for jazz choir."

I walked in, and I worked with the jazz choir. Russ smiles."

"Next period musical theatre."

I worked with the musical theatre kids. He smiles."

"Next period is girls' choir."

Afterwards, he said, "All right, you are hired."

"I wasn't looking for a job."

"You have one now."

For three years, I got paid to go over in the morning and be an assistant with jazz, musical theatre, and girls' choir. I would go to college classes, bust my butt until 10:00 p.m., and then do it again. Russ was amazing and fun to work with. Then he got Gary Frame's job. I couldn't figure Russ out; he was low key and intense at the same time. He was not a holy terror in the classroom at all. It was like a constant fifty-five. He is an extraordinary guy. The kids loved him.

Russ took the Sprague job as I was coming into my student teaching. I had been in a four-year program and decided to go for five. I volunteered for a year at McKay. Graber said, "You can student teach with me, but you have to volunteer for a year," so I did that and got to student teach.

Graber was the polar opposite of Russ. Russ would be calm and say, "That was super disappointing." Someone would make a mistake at McKay, and Chuck would slam his hand on the piano. "Stand up! Do it again." And the kids would stand up, and Chuck would solo test kids. "Stand up, sing for me." BAM! "Sing for me." BAM! The energy level. The ninja warrior up there, just chopping people. I think I am definitely more like Chuck in my teaching. Chuck and my dad were similar in style, very energetic, very "go at the kids," high bar. It was okay for Chuck to be tense and tough with the kids, because they knew he loved them. He honestly cared about them.

These are the experiences I grew up in. Then I taught for four years at Seaside, straight from Western Oregon University to Seaside. I had no master's yet, but I had the five-year license that was required at the time. I loved Seaside. I started with thirty-five kids and left with 280. I had half the school in my program. It was amazing. Neil Priddy was the science teacher there, a guy who was phenomenal, an archer for the US Olympic team, a University of Washington engineer who helped develop the tri-robotic finger, who was a multimillionaire but no one knew it. He had all this land he bought for Nature Conservancy, an extraordinary guy. He basically retired at thirty-five and he was teaching just to work with kids. The day I left, Neil looked at me and said, "You are going to regret leaving this job for the rest of your career. This is the place," and he was right. I have yet to land anywhere where the impact of my engagement was as vital to their future as at Seaside. Seaside had 550 kids, low income. We would transition in and out 30 to 40 percent of our kids every year and always have the same population at the end of the year. It was insane in and out, because it was a resort town, so you have this high turnover with parents. A good 25 to 35 percent had a solid income and the rest were very poor, but I loved working there. We were state champs in football and track; we had unbelievable success with the kids. We had a great group and plenty of nature. We would have faculty days when we were grading, but we were out at the Astoria Pier 8 buoy, crabbing, having a clam bake with all the families. You just couldn't pass it up. The salmon fishing was spectacular.

I then decided to go to grad school. Many, many conductors in the northwest have been trained under Maurice Skones. He had been at the University of Arizona for fifteen to twenty years. He started his career at Pacific Lutheran, which is why I wanted to go to Pacific Lutheran because of the choral program he had built there. So I was at U of A, and I actually applied to go there just as Maurice retired—he retired when I arrived. I was involved with the person who replaced him and thought it would still be a strong program, but it disintegrated in the first year. And so the gentleman was moved out and Skones came back, and I got to do two out of three year's work with Maurice. He came out of retirement and stayed there for an additional seven years. He passed away right after he retired for good.

The University of Arizona experience was outstanding, but I arrived in the midst of disruption. Basically four grad students were promised the same scholarship, all accepted and we all showed up. There was only one scholarship. Having four scholarships was bad management by the person who replaced Skones. In an effort to recruit people, he promised what wasn't available, so we got farmed out to other areas and since my other great passion was jazz, I was assigned to the jazz department. In a matter of months, I went from an unsure situation to being the assistant director of jazz at the University of Arizona. I taught a jazz history program and had 650 to 750 kids in my class every semester. I taught jazz history, built up a vocal jazz program, instituted a small elite a capella group, which I had also done at Western Oregon, and that elite group became the backup group for Linda Ronstadt.

That is when I started working with Linda on and off for seven years. She lived in Tucson and was a Tucson native. Hence, in Tucson there were massive amounts of recordings taking place. We did recordings in the studios for advertisements and soundtracks. I worked with Linda either on stage or in the sound booth, and at the same time, I was the librarian for the jazz program, taking in material that was coming in from donors, working with the Artie Shaw Library named after the band leader. *Begin the Beguine* is probably his most famous piece. I worked with Nelson Riddle's Library, which was brought to us via Linda Ronstadt and our jazz head, Jeff Haskell, and Rob Cutietta, Director of the School of Music and Dance at the University. They worked with Nelson Riddle's family and were able to obtain all of that material.

I was in everything, doing everything. I was singing in a classical choir, conducting two jazz groups, singing in a professional jazz group, conducting a boys' choir across town, officiated as the artistic and musical director for the Reveille Gay Men's Chorus, and doing a church gig. I was in the studio at 2:00 a.m. when they needed to get an advertisement out by 8:00 a.m. the next morning. When I was in LA for a vacation, I received a phone call that said "come back, we are going to be in the studio for four weeks." It became this Mad Hatter madness; my fingers were in everything, and I was studying classical conducting at the same time. It was nothing for me to be up at 2:00 to 3:00 a.m. every morning rehearsing, recording, writing, editing, arranging for bass players, pianists, and drummers. That was the world I was immersed in. I did collapse, lost a marriage, became a heavy drinker, suffered a second failed relationship with a woman who I thought would have been wife number two. There was lots of madness in those years. After seven and a half years there, I was exhausted.

When I was on tour in San Francisco, I met a woman I had gone to high school with who was also in Gary Frame's choir. We connected and married six months later, married for twelve years, and that ended five years ago. I was married for twenty-four years, just not to the same woman, not all in one span.

All these extra hours, my addiction to teaching and music making, the core of all my professional work in some way, shape, or form had driven me until this year. When I came to Claggett Creek, it didn't matter to the principal, Rob Schoepper what I taught, only that I was a good teacher. First you are a good teacher and then you become expert at one or two subjects, but I believe a great teacher can teach any subject. That was drilled into me by my family and relatives who were all teachers.

My positions at Claggett Creek were a matter of timing. When I decided I was done teaching at the high school, I was advised to stop doing anything that would make my life more miserable. On a Sunday night, I filled out an application and sent emails out to twelve to fifteen middle school principals that I was available. I didn't want to do music. But I wanted to do electives. Rob Schoepper from Claggett Creek called me right away. "Hey, I have a great group of kids here. We have a need for more elective classes. We have massive requests for foods and sewing. Our sewing teacher does sewing and foods. She could emphasize more sewing, and we could move more foods to you. We lost drama five years ago, but we could bring it back." And Rob really wanted video production at his school. As Rob and I were talking, we knew McNary has great drama and I had been in theatre my whole life. I have been cooking since I was a child. McNary has a great audio/video production program and I ran the audio side working along-side video all the time, so it was very easy for me to say, "Let's do those three things." Rob wanted the kids to have a daily news broadcast, so we brainstormed together. He wanted things that translated to programs in high school that translated to college and careers. We daydreamed over a couple of meetings, and he had the space. Tons of kids were interested. The numbers were ridiculous, so I teach five classes a semester, a combination of drama, video production and food.I think the foods class is so fun. We made biscuits in foods class. I had six teams of six kids. Each team did their own biscuit recipe and then they traded biscuits so they could taste them and compare. Some were savory, some sweet, good ol' southern biscuits. The kids were in heaven. All the broadcasts, the cooking, the drama—I never have any discipline problems. I do not have kids of my own. That is one of my biggest regrets, but I often tell the kids, "You are my kids. You are my passion."

The Swan Family

In 1984, Delia Miller, representing the local Lutheran Fine Arts program, was eating lunch in downtown Salem when she noticed Dr. Wallace Long sitting at a nearby table. He was the new choir director at Willamette University; Miller had been impressed with his choirs she had seen on campus. She struck up a conversation with Long and suggested that he could be the conductor of a brand new choir in Salem. The Lutheran Fine Arts would be the sponsor.

It was a community choir; anyone could be in it; there were no auditions. In fact, in the beginning, it was called the Willamette University Community Choir, a name that was warm and welcoming. At the same time, there were certain people like me who probably shouldn't have been in it. We couldn't sight-read as well as others and didn't have the proper tone quality.

That has all changed. Long became so busy with his work at the university that he handed over the reins to Dr. Paul Klemme, who has been director of what is now called the Willamette Master Chorus for over twenty years. A truly accomplished man, Klemme is music director for *the* music church in town, St. Paul's Episcopal Church. Not only is he good at directing choir, but he is a skilled pianist and organist. In his role with the Willamette Master Chorus, he requires auditions—not only auditions but re-auditions. Everyone in the choir must re-audition every three years to stay in the Chorus.

Because of Klemme's policy, there is constant turnover, but the level of ability continually improves. There are people who re-audition and don't make it. About three years before I talked with members of the Swan family, the choir lost about half of the alto section through re-auditions; half of the section was now new. Half a dozen to two dozen people will drop out of the choir, possibly because of personal circumstances but also because they don't feel confident in a re-audition. This wholesale change can cause minor upheaval in the beginning, but soon people settle in. People get used to new people and develop new relationships. At present, the chorus has about eighty members.

No one in the choir is paid, but with the upgrading, the Willamette Master Chorus has become semiprofessional. Many music teachers from the Salem-Keizer School District have been a part at one time or another. The group periodically tours, often to Europe. Expectations in rehearsals are high. Klemme has a policy that after the first read-through, he is not going to teach notes any more. He doesn't want to spend rehearsal time running over sections with people struggling on something; he expects all to learn it outside. He will have sectionals and say, "I would like section leaders to go from this page to this page for this particular work, and make sure everyone in your section knows it or knows what they need to work on." This happens typically before that piece is introduced to the entire choir for rehearsal. By the second read-through, the chorus is working on dynamics and phrasing.

With this rigor, it would be an achievement for two members of a family to pass a re-audition. In the history of the Chorus, there have been spouses, a parent and child, siblings, but with the entrance of the Swans, for the first time, the chorus has been blessed with an entire nuclear family: Michael, his wife, Diane, their daughter, Caitlin, and their son, Ryan. Michael and Caitlin auditioned first and have each auditioned three times. Diane and Ryan came later and have auditioned twice. When I met with the Swans in May of 2017, all four were scheduled for re-auditions the following August.

Michael feels more sorry for Klemme than for any member of his family, thinking, "What happens if one of us doesn't make it? That would be awkward for Paul." Michael also expects that if one doesn't survive the re-audition, the other three will continue in the Chorus.

Each of the four Swans have traveled a unique musical road to the chorus:

Michael graduated from North High School in 1972 during a time when there were only two other high schools in the district: South and McNary. If the area feeding into North was not as impoverished as it is now, it was still working-class Salem. There were pockets of upper-middle-class living, particularly among folks out in the country. When the free and reduced lunch program came in; Michael doubts the eligibility was much higher than 30 percent.

Michael never chose music as a career—he majored in chemistry and is now a retired civil engineer. He came from a family of seven members—five kids; both parents were musicians. His father was a percussionist and his mother played piano. In addition, his great-grandmother, Hallie Watson Millsap, was a graduate in music from Willamette University in 1905, a time when there were few women at Willamette. She was Michael's mother's piano teacher. His parents expected that all the kids would play a musical instrument. Both of his sisters played the piano, his two brothers played wind instruments, and Michael played the flute.

Michael's band instructor at Waldo Junior High was Grant Hagestedt, a fixture in Salem for many years and a legend of sorts. I first met him when he was teaching at Judson. He is still a member of St. Paul's Episcopal Church and Michael is Facebook friends with him. Michael says,

> Grant is the person who taught me the only formal instruction I ever had on music theory—the latest in 1969—so it has faded from my memory a great deal. I played flute at Washington Elementary and Waldo and then dropped it, although I still own the flute.

From then on and for decades, even when attending Oregon State University, Michael was surrounded by music but not producing it. Listening to music might have been the first thing he did in his life. He has an early memory of Smetana's *Moldau*, likely on the only record the family owned for many years. He still listens to music every day.

> I have an eclectic mix of bluegrass to psychedelic rock-and-roll to country to classical, which includes chamber music, symphonic music and choral music. My current favorite—and has been for years—is Renaissance. I love nothing better than a quartet or a sextet singing Palestrina's *Victoria.*

Michael sang off and on because music had always been a part of his life, but he was never in a choir until Diane and the director at Jason Lee United Methodist Church, Wendy Bemrose, recruited him during Advent in 1992 because they needed another bass. Michael said,

> At that point, as someone who had played the flute, yes, I knew what music was. I could read a treble clef, but the bass clef was foreign to me. I had to learn to read bass clef and learn to sing as part of a group, which was completely different from anything I had done before. Playing an instrument in a group is different from singing in a group. When I play the flute, if I push down the correct key, I get that tone. There is a little bit of wiggle room, depending on embouchure, but when I sing, my vocal folds and tracks are all I have to produce a note. It is not fixed, not as simple as pushing down certain keys, so the combination of ears, voice, my entire body, and breathing all affect the tone and the pitch of what I am doing. For someone who has been an instrumentalist, singing is harder than playing an instrument. Don't get me wrong. Playing an instrument at a professional level is quite a challenge and a lot of work, but for me personally, singing has taken more effort to reproduce notes on pitch.

Diane, like her husband, did not have a career in music, but she did something related. She taught English and public speaking at Sprague High School for eighteen years and then moved to the district to become a program assistant. She works in the curriculum department, teaching other teachers and administrators. In that sense, she does public speaking for a living.

Diane grew up in northeast Salem on what is now 45th Street: "Very rural," she said. Some of the nearby neighborhoods she described as posh, but as the houses aged over the past sixty to seventy years, a good number became rentals, bringing the socioeconomics downward. She countered, "There are nice housing developments in this area too." She went to Middle Grove Elementary, Waldo Junior High, and Whiteaker Junior High the year it opened. She might have gone to McKay High, but there was no McKay then, so she went to McNary. Even McNary was relatively new; her brother was in the first graduating class of 1966. Diane graduated in 1972, the same year as Michael.

Diane's mother had the opportunity to take a few piano lessons as a child, but because her experience had been limited, she was determined that all her children would have access to music lessons.

> That piano right there (the old upright in their home) is the one I inherited from my aunt, and when I took piano lessons, that was the piano I played on. I was six when I started, but I wasn't very good. I didn't practice enough, of course, but I took lessons off and on for six or seven years. Because of the lessons, I could read music.

Diane sang in choirs beginning in junior high and continuing through high school and college.

> I always sang in choirs. I was not planning on being a music major, but I loved singing. I wanted that in my life, so singing in the concert choir at Oregon College of Education (now Western

Oregon University) was my elective. Dr. Ron Wynn was the choral director there during the 1970s. I was also in the chorus for some musicals. I did *Man of La Mancha* in college and later *Oklahoma* at the Pentacle Community Theatre in Salem. I loved choral music, loved singing with people. Then after the kids were young and we were going to church at Jason Lee, I joined the choir there and eventually got Michael to join. They needed a bass, and he discovered that he enjoyed singing, so he stuck around.

My musicianship has grown significantly. The year we lost a number of altos in the Willamette Master Chorus, I had started voice lessons with Cynthia McGladrey, and that may be one of the reasons I was not one of the altos who was replaced. I was working very hard on my vocal abilities, my musicianship, although I still suffer from stage fright when I sing a solo and I competed in public speaking in college! Playing the piano in front of people or when I am trying to accompany someone is even worse than singing, ten times worse than speaking in public. I don't mind singing solos, but I don't live to do it. Singing solos doesn't make Michael particularly anxious anymore either, but public speaking does.

THE SWAN'S OLDER CHILD, RYAN, GREW UP IN NORTHEAST SALEM in the house where his parents still live. He went to school at Scott Elementary and middle school at Adams Stephens the year it opened (Stephens opened the year before, but only because Parrish was being remodeled. It was crowded because all the Parrish kids were there). Ryan graduated from McKay High School in 2002 and graduated from St. Martin's University in Washington.

Ryan was in the choir at Scott Elementary; he said,

> I remembered standing in front of students, but I don't remember ever choosing to be in the choir. My parents did that for me. I sang at church, because there were enough youth at Jason Lee for a youth choir. I was a boy soprano in the elementary.

Michael said, "We had great hopes he would be a tenor so our family could be SATB (soprano, alto, tenor, bass), but Ryan was a tenor for about two weeks."

Ryan picked up the clarinet in the fifth grade despite the skepticism of his band teacher. He said,

> We went through listening to the four instruments offered: flute, clarinet, trumpet, and trombone. We then tooted on the mouthpieces to see which one we wanted to play. I heard the clarinet, liked it, tried it out, but the band teacher asked if I was sure that was the instrument I wanted to pick. I said yes. She said, "Are you sure? Because of the way your mouth is shaped, you will never be any good at it." Well, in middle school, I was in the band, still playing clarinet, and in the eighth grade, I was in the jazz band playing tenor sax. In high school, I did marching band all four years; Jaimie Hall was the teacher. I did not get into the jazz band my first year, but I got into the Wind Ensemble by the skin of my teeth. Mr. Hall put me on bass clarinet.

The area around McKay High School, which Ryan and Caitlin attended, was not as impoverished as it is now. Michael said,

> What has changed is the number of multifamily apartments filling in, and then you have the problem with any section of town as it gets older. It ages, the houses are older, and some don't stay in good repair and are smaller proportionately than the McMansions that are being built on the outskirts of town, mostly near Sprague and West, whereas here in the northeast, much of the land out of town has continued to be more agricultural, so we don't have the McMansions at this end of town. Part of it is zoning, and we don't have the hills. People with money seem to want to live in the hills.

Ryan said,

> McKay was in the lower end of the socioeconomic scale when I graduated in 2002, but I remember that our band program was entirely fundraised. The only thing the district was paying for was teachers' salaries. All of the bussing, instrument repairs, all

> was covered through fundraising. We had a very active booster group; they were able to do a lot with the money that was given them. The booster group didn't just support the jazz band or wind ensemble, but much of that money went into school owned instruments and maintenance. We went to a lot of competitions that were outside the normal circuit, and when I was a sophomore and senior, we fundraised for the band and orchestra to take a trip to Disneyland for the Heritage Music Festival.

Ryan became active in band during high school; he was in the marching band and the Wind Ensemble. By his sophomore year, Ryan was in the jazz band and the pep band during basketball season. He was in the pit band for musicals and the lower band when they needed to fill out a section. He was in the All-City band for three years, took over his dad's flute, and played that and the clarinet in the jazz band. He also played in the West Coast Honor Band, a large band based out of Seattle.

The band professor at Willamette University, Martin Behnke, recruited Ryan to play at the university graduation commencement. He had been on the panel for the All-City auditions during Ryan's junior year when Behnke had half of his clarinet section study abroad. That fall, Behnke invited five students recommended by the band directors involved in the All-City auditions to play in the Willamette Wind Ensemble, the university's upper-level band. Ryan was recommended and the only one who was accepted to be in the band. He played with the university band his entire high school senior year. He was invited back to play for the university commencement twice: once on the clarinet and once on the tenor sax. He had a music scholarship when he went to college.

And this for a kid whose elementary teacher thought he would never be any good at the clarinet and who never liked to practice. Ryan said,

> I could have been first chair if I had ever practiced outside the classroom, but I never did. The first chair student in the Wind Ensemble was both talented and hard-working. I just skated by on talent.

That had been his father's problem with the flute: when Michael was in junior high, he was first or second chair all the time, but he never practiced.

Ryan went to college at a small school where half the band was from the college and half from the community. He said,

> We were playing charts I played in middle school; I lost interest in playing my instrument there, because I was unchallenged. Besides, I didn't go to St. Martins to be a music major. At the time, I didn't think I was good enough nor was I dedicated enough to make a profession out of it. I didn't consider being a teacher. In college, I took theory courses, picked up the piano a little bit and that was all.

During this time, Ryan was involved with choir. Through high school, he was in his church choir, and in college, he was doing band and choir simultaneously. He said that being an instrumentalist taught him a lot about rhythm and sight-reading; being a vocalist taught him about other things such as tone and blend. After he quit playing wind instruments, he did more with vocal in school, and after college, he moved back to Salem and got back into church choir: first Jason Lee and then First United Methodist. Neither was especially challenging, but he was there because he needed some outlet and because he had a certain institutional loyalty to the group.

Caitlin Swan Clark is the only soloist of the family in the Willamette Master Chorus—in fact, the only family member to audition to be a soloist. The other members did solos elsewhere but not with WMC. She has one other interesting tick on her life's resume: she was married in 2012, and one year later, she and her husband spent their anniversary in France when a subset of the Chorus sang at a festival in Paris. The group also performed in several towns and cities throughout the country. Her husband is a high school math teacher in the district. She said, "He can't carry a tune in a bucket, but I love him dearly."

Like Ryan, Caitlin was surrounded by music early.

> There was always music in the house, various kinds of music from Weird Al to classical. What I learned from Weird Al was that you can really mess with the words in songs and they can still be good. He does lots of parodies. I sang in the small church choir at Jason Lee and did youth musicals. I loved being on stage and I still do. At Scott Elementary, Ryan and I got our first taste of playing a recorder and the xylophone, although playing the xylophone was not as much fun for me.

Caitlin joined the orchestra in fourth grade.

> Bruce Purdy was the teacher; we run into him every now and then. He sometimes plays bass for the First United Methodist Church choir and occasionally for the Willamette Master Chorus. When I first heard the band and orchestra instruments, I was trying to decide between the viola and the cello. I was thinking about it, but I have never been a large person with particularly long fingers. My concern was that my hands were not going to be big enough for the cello. There are longer strings, and you have to get your hand around the neck with proper finger position and the cello—even a small cello—was a lot bigger than I was in the fourth grade. I chose the viola over the violin also because the violin was too screechy. In elementary school, we used tape, special tape on the neck of the instrument or smiley face stickers to tell us where our fingers belonged depending on where the normal finger position was, usually the key of C.

Purdy was Caitlin's teacher through the eighth grade. At Stephens Middle School, she was in the intermediate orchestra, usually in first or second chair.

> Sean Williams did student teaching with us. He was a viola guy and I thought that was really cool. He had this enormous viola and I thought, I can't play that thing! I was not playing a full-sized viola. I had a violin strung as a viola and didn't have a real viola until I was in high school.

Caitlin graduated from McKay in 2004. She was in the top orchestra from her sophomore through her senior year. She said,

> I was usually first chair, not because I practiced the most. The second chair violist always felt that she deserved it, because she practiced more than I did. (Michael added, "All four of us have been bad about practicing.") I was one of those terrible people who would look over something, go through it a few times, and I smoked the other girl every time. I felt bad but not bad enough to practice.

In middle school, Caitlin was deluged with activities. She was in the jazz choir and the top concert choir from the time she was in the sixth grade. Manny McGladrey was her director. She was in orchestra, musicals, plays, and even sang in a talent show. Her teacher, Lucas Anderson, was a past member of Willamette Master Chorus (Ryan stood next to him). Caitlin sang in choir at McKay as well, but her experience there was mixed. One director left last minute and new directors were still auditioning at the beginning of her senior year. Her new teacher became Eugene Rogers, lately from the Harlem Boys Choir. Caitlin and Rogers did not get along terribly well. She said,

> I did not have the sound he was looking for in a soprano voice. He was a tough teacher; the only positive thing I got from him was that I was chosen as soloist for the Christmas concert and the concert shortly before my graduation. If he chose me as soloist, he must have trusted my abilities as a musician, but in choir, he kept moving me down. I had been a first soprano and then he would move me to second soprano and on some pieces, he had me sing alto. I joked that I was just waiting for him to move me to tenor so he couldn't hear me at all. I know that I have a very bright and clear sound. I don't think I was always good at managing that and making it blend nicely with people around me. That was our biggest musical issue.

Despite her challenges, Caitlin was in a choir and orchestra that went to the state competition when she was a senior. She enrolled in Willamette University, the only person in her family to become a music major. She became more passionate about singing than playing the viola—she took voice lessons from McGladrey in high school—and knew she would not have time for both. She dropped viola and concentrated on vocal and joined the choir.

She liked the choral director, Dr. Wallace Long.

> He is fun to work with but also very demanding. He and Paul Klemme have a way of communicating their expectations and what they are looking for from their singers without becoming negative, which is a very valuable skill. Not all directors choose to do that.

Caitlin had less favorable results with several voice teachers until her junior year when she started taking lessons from Les Green. "He was a phenomenal tenor who literally sings all over the world. He and I worked well together. After studying with him, I qualified to be a performance major."

Caitlin earned a double major in vocal performance and music education.

> But in my senior year, either Les was sick or I was sick, and I didn't have many voice lessons. I dropped the performance major and needed an extra semester to complete my credits. I officially got my degree in December of 2009 but couldn't immediately go into the ed program. I ended up putting it off when all the layoffs were happening and I wasn't even sure I wanted to be in it. I didn't go into the master's program, but I enjoy kids, did classroom studies with local orchestra teachers, some choir teachers, and found that I love elementary music. It has always been on my mind to go back and get my master's to teach elementary, but when I met my husband in 2011, he and I talked and decided it made more sense, since both of us wanted to have kids in the near future, to put off getting my master's until after we had our kids. Right now, I want to be a stay-at-home mom.

YEARS AGO, THERE WAS A MUSIC STORE IN SALEM CALLED OPUS One. One of the employees, Mike Whalen, had been a member of the Willamette Master Chorus since its inception.

Whalen had known Michael and tried to recruit him to join the group without ever having heard him sing. He did this because of Caitlin going to Willamette. She sang with the top choir at Willamette, the Chamber Choir, which was often invited to sing with the Master Chorus for major works such as *Creation* or *Messiah.* (Ryan said, "There is a marked difference between an 80-voice choir and a 120- to 150-voice choir trying to compete with a large orchestra.")

Michael said,

> Because of being exposed to programs, which included Wallace Long and Paul Klemme, I got to know them a little bit. Caitlin and I talked about it and thought we would audition. The two of us auditioned the same year in 2009; Caitlin walked the graduation but had one semester left. I knew Willamette Master Chorus existed, but I had not been to more than one or two concerts. I was feeling that I had reached the growth I could achieve in the church choir and the a capella group I belonged to. I needed some additional challenge. In terms of instruction, I felt like a big fish in a small pond to being a small fish in a very large pond by moving to the Willamette Master Chorus. It really was a lot of additional work, but I worked really hard, and I still work hard, but I don't have to struggle quite as much. My musicianship has grown as a result of being a member of the group.

Later, Diane and Ryan auditioned and were accepted into the choir. Ryan said, "It is a challenging group and brought me back to 'Oh, this is what music is like—not easy.'"

Three months later, I called the Swans to see how they fared with their re-auditions. They all passed and are members of the Willamette Master Chorus for at least three more years.

Walt Farrier

Walt Farrier is one of the most all-around gifted musicians I know. He has a long history in teaching and performing (vocal and instrumental), composing, arranging and music theory, but he is far more than music. He is kind, always willing to help others when he can. For years, he took care of his wife, Joan, until her passing after fifty-nine years of marriage. She was a woman of great insight and humor but also plagued with unending physical hardships.

Farrier is also one of the most brilliant people I have ever met. In addition to music, he can wax on about medicine, the human body, and a host of other subjects to a greater or lesser degree (he cannot name every shrub and flower in our yard).

If Farrier is familiar with medicine, it is because in 1950, he was a new undergraduate at Yale University, intending to become a psychiatrist. Getting into Yale was as difficult then as it is now, even more so for women (Yale was still an all-male school). One student was accepted for every twenty-eight who applied. For Farrier, it was much slimmer than that. Of all the students at Yale, 74 percent came from private prep schools. Walt was from a public school.

Becoming a psychiatrist required going to medical school followed by a residency. If being accepted into Yale was difficult, getting into medical school was worse. There were fewer medical schools per capita than now. Fifty students applied for each one chosen, but Farrier was accepted at the University of Pennsylvania Medical School. He was sure he was on his way to an eminent career. He was fascinated by the subject matter and was in good academic standing.

But he soon realized he had a major weakness. In residency, he would have to perform minor surgery such as removing a mole or a cyst. He would have to inject a patient. He said,

> To become a psychiatrist, you had to become an MD. It was an absolute requirement in residency to handle people with serious injuries. The school had films in color on a big screen in a small auditorium, and as we watched them do the operation from start to finish, we would take notes. I remembered so well writing as fast as I could as the soundtrack informed us what was happening, why this layer had to be removed or that layer retained to heal the surface. At the end of the fifty-minute film, my left hand was so tight I literally couldn't open it. I had to pry each finger open rather painfully; my body was telling me this was not what I should be doing for a living. I am one of these people who to this day can't stand to watch a violent or gory movie. When *Spartacus* came out, I had to leave the room. I quit med school in the middle of the first year. It made me so tense seeing someone sliced open, and I realized I couldn't do it. I felt guilty leaving medical school, because getting in was even more selective than Yale, but I don't think I would have liked medicine better than music anyway. Music was always my first love.

FARRIER GREW UP IN MAPLEWOOD, NEW JERSEY, ON THE OUTSKIRTS of metropolitan New York City. His mother had trained at Juilliard and sung lead operatic roles in the New York Opera Company. His father was an accountant who became comptroller of Bloomingdale's in New York. The city of Maplewood had a population of 23,239 according to the 1950 census. Farrier said,

> It is much bigger now and not nearly as wealthy. There was no countryside anywhere nearby—this was New Jersey. You cross a traffic light, and you are in the next town. Most people commuted; it was a commuter town. New Jersey is still the most densely populated state. If you were going to the next town, how many traffic lights would that be? The idea of fields in between just didn't happen.

Crime was rampant in much of New Jersey, which in a way made music more important. Farrier said,

> There was a New Jersey saying: "Teach a boy to blow a horn, and he will never blow a safe." The result was that New Jersey had enormous programs although not so much in the public schools and not anywhere near what we have here in Salem, but my own musical education was good. By grade three, the teacher gave us little tonettes, plastic knockoffs that looked like recorders but shorter so kids could carry them. By the second half of the third grade, if a child was doing pretty well, he was given a metal version of a recorder, and in the fourth grade, we began on real instruments. I started playing saxophone, accomplished enough to be chosen as a soloist for assembly programs. I was fortunate to have one very good teacher in instrumental music, an excellent trumpet player named Harold Rudy. He did some performing, but mostly he directed all the bands in the junior high and high school.

Rudy's mentorship was critical in making it possible for Farrier and another student to start a band in the sixth grade.

> In the sixth grade, we weren't playing in public, but we were meeting and playing; already I was starting to write arrangements. In the seventh grade, we started playing for pay. With slightly different personnel, our band called Starry Knights continued together all the way through high school. We had a very good trumpet player and pianist and I played mostly saxophone but also the clarinet. My partner was the music director and I was the business person. We didn't have too many gigs in the seventh grade, but beginning in eighth grade, we performed maybe eight to ten times a year, making five dollars apiece each time, which was big money in those days. By the time we were seniors in high school, we had at least ten gigs a year pulling in as much as ten dollars apiece per gig. We started out with school events, but even in the eighth grade, we were playing for weddings and bar mitzvahs. In high school, it was a country club dance or something similar. The musicians' union was prominent in New Jersey, but they didn't go after us when we were in junior high and high school.

Farrier played in the band at Yale University; he showed me pictures of him playing in the pit orchestras for musicals. He was also a disc jockey on the Yale radio station, but his claim to fame would be with choir. Male singing groups were important at Yale, because the school was all male until 1979 and involved far more people than band. In 1952, when Farrier was a sophomore, he and two others founded a men's group called The Duke's Men, named after the master of his residential college, Duke Henning.

> Before the first year was over, we were taking singers from other colleges. (He showed me pictures.) The Duke's Men still exists and has an alumni association to this day. I still correspond with some of the people in that group. Although most of the founders are dead now, the group is still very active. They take two-week vacations in the Bahamas and generally do a lot of traveling.

Farrier was the musical director for The Duke's Men and composed music for them.

> They sang a number of my original compositions, but mostly I did arrangements. I did nineteen arrangements for them of well-known tunes. We played some very good gigs and were good enough to get into a contest involving eight to ten groups. These competitions were held in a big auditorium every year among all these male groups; our group came in second my senior year and first the next year. We were singing mostly my arrangements. The words were original. One time I made a silly spoof of *Tea for Two*—the second verse was *Tea for Three:*
>
> *Please tell your brother to take off and leave us alone!*
> *We can't make out until he takes his pet snake out;*
> *He thinks he's so cute in his Buck Rogers suit,*
> *Now he's pouring molasses all over my glasses—remove him!!*
> *Can't you see that I am a wreck—let's hang this kid so we can—"dance."*
> *Can't you see how happy we could be! Happy, shall we be!*
> *When this kid hangs from a tree!!*
>
> There was a senior male group called the Wiffenpoofs, which drew from all the other college groups. I almost made it into that,

but I learned later on I didn't because in those days it was for the socially elite. There was a class system at Yale. Most of the students went to private prep schools, but our singing group was fortunate enough to still do well in the contests.

When Farrier dropped out of medical school, he knew his days as a civilian would be few. Although the Korean War had concluded and was winding down, the army was still drafting males. Before being drafted, he thought if he could audition, he would get into an army band. He said,

> My local recruiting officer arranged for me to go down and take an audition in the few days before the draft notice came, but he said my chance of getting into an army band was zero unless I signed up for the regular army, which is a four-year stint. I believed him, of course, and went down to audition at Fort Dix for the Headquarters Army band. I passed the audition, but while I was waiting in the office for the audition, I heard two company clerks calling lists of people across the aisle between their two desks identifying guys by their army serial number. Some numbers began with RA and some with US, and as I listened to this for a few minutes, I wondered what the difference was. I asked the clerk, "What is the difference between RA and US? They all have the same number of digits after the letters." He said, "Oh yeah, very simple. The RAs are regular army, people who have enlisted for four years. The USs are draftees who are in for two years." "Well, what was the percentage of guys in the band from both categories?" "About fifty-fifty," so the recruiting officer had lied to me, or else he didn't know. After I passed the audition, the officer who auditioned me said, "If you go down two buildings on the right-hand side, you can sign, and you will become a US Army bandsman right then and there. After you finish basic training, there will be a sign for the band." I said, "Before I go over and sign up for four years, I want to do this in my home area." I realized I didn't have to do this for four years. The recruiting officer said fine. He gave me a paper showing that I had passed the audition. I then went home and waited for the draft.
>
> When the draft came, I had to go through basic training, but

I had the letter saying I had been accepted to play in the First Headquarters Army band, and now I would only be in for two years. The First Headquarters Army band didn't need any sax players, but the Third Army Band in Georgia did. I went to Fort Benning, which is a big infantry basic training area in Georgia and played in that band for six to eight months. I was in the stage band playing for dances and I did arrangements for the music we played. We still had to go on maneuvers, turning the band into a labor detail. We were digging latrines, putting up tents, taking down tents, standing nighttime guard duty. We didn't get to play at all on maneuvers.

During this time, I arranged on a pass to audition for the Third Army Headquarters band stationed at Fort McPherson (it was closed in 2011). Fort McPherson was in Atlanta at the edge of the city. I passed that audition and got transferred to the Headquarters Army band and that was glorious! I wish I had a picture of that band. People who played in the Headquarters Army band were real pros. I was fortunate enough to play with them. We had five trombones and good ones; two of them went directly from that band to the Denver Symphony and Dallas Symphony. One had played with Les Brown. There were five trumpets who were excellent and five saxes, all of whom played both sax and clarinet. By then, I had picked up the flute, which I had a chance to learn at Fort Benning.

At Fort McPherson, the stage band did a recruiting broadcast every week going through many of my arrangements. I was writing arrangements as fast as I could, because the band recorded on tapes—everything was on tape in those days. The stage band went through a substantial number of charts, some of them mine. We had, in addition to the five trumpets, five trombones and five saxes, four French horns and they were good! One of the French horn players was first horn for Frederick Fennell in the Eastman Wind Ensemble. I was able to arrange for wind combinations such as four horns and four flutes, a sound that was fresh, because people hadn't heard four horns and four flutes played together, something stage bands had never had before. One arrangement I made was for a large series of charts called *The Nutcracker Unsweetened,* a seven- or eight-movement jazz version of The Nutcracker Suite with the last note of a line goofy. The opening movement was called *Walt's of the Flowers.* It was a kick to do that. I was in the Headquarters Army band for the remainder of my two years, getting discharged from the army in March of 1957.

When Farrier was discharged from the military, he played professionally and took piano lessons, all back in New Jersey.

I played in small combos in places like bars in Newark, literally *on* bars; the piano was in the pit, but the bass, drums, percussion and instruments were on the bar. I played the sax—alternating between alto and tenor sax—clarinet and flute. The money was pretty good, but the musicians' union was strict and to be in the union cost $200, which was a lot of money then. It would be around $2,000 now. There was the $200 initiation fee, the $200 yearly dues, but the joker was that you couldn't play anywhere initially for six months. I never knew why I couldn't play for six months, but that was part of the rules. I was not allowed to play; I couldn't afford that and even though I was a member of the musician's union in the area where I lived, the good jobs demanded that I be in the New York union.

I decided to play scab gigs. It wasn't really legal, so whenever I played at a place, a union rep would soon come by—there were always two guys: a weaselly little guy, usually with his nose off center, and a great big moose, always wearing a double-breasted, pink-striped, blue suit and a tie that didn't go with it at all. They would talk with the owner of the bar, the owner sitting down and the weaselly guy across from him. The bruiser would stand next to the owner and as far as I could tell, he never said anything. After they left, the owner would tell us, "We can't hire you after tonight or after this weekend." We were always scheduled to play Friday, Saturday, and Sunday nights. What was so strange is that wherever we went, it was never the same weaselly guy. They weren't the same pair in each place, but they all looked like they came from the same central casting unit. The moose always wore a tie that didn't go with the suit. The weaselly guy didn't usually wear a suit. He would have a jacket with an open white shirt. Someone picked them out of a cartoon.

The unions were not connected to the mafia, but they were pretty thorough. I was fortunate that I never got my tires slashed or my instrument stolen or trashed; things like that did happen. I am talking about Newark. In those days, Newark was not the tightly controlled law enforcement setup it is now. Newark was the only city I was ever in that had no nice part, not any nice part. The parks had wrought iron fences all around them. They were locking them up at night, even in 1950 when I was a senior in high school, because there were so many muggings.

I played gigs after I got out of service for fifteen months, but I also taught school. This because of help by a friend of mine who had played with Glen Miller and was now selling musical instruments for George Schirmer in downtown New York. He was their New Jersey agent for schools, but he also lined up places where schools needed instrument instructors. At that time schools were very short on instructors partly because so many people were still in the army. I got what was known as an emergency certification: if I could show enough instrumental performance competency and had a college degree, I could legally teach instrumental music in schools if the administrators had trouble finding regular music education graduates for teaching.

I was playing gigs anywhere in New Jersey, even up by the Pennsylvania or New York borders, staying one step ahead of the union. I was also teaching at seven different schools, six of them on Monday through Wednesday, sometimes two schools a day. On Thursday and Friday, I was teaching at a school near the Pennsylvania border, a hundred-mile round trip. Unfortunately, I had to be back on Thursday night, because I was a paid singer at a church. I was also still learning how to play the piano. For fifteen months, I was playing, teaching, rehearsing at church on Thursday nights, and singing for two services on Sundays. I was getting to bed at 1:00 a.m. on Fridays and Saturdays only to sing on Sunday mornings, while putting 343 miles a week in transportation. I realized I had to cut down on something in order to survive. What I cut out was the combo, which paid six times as much as teaching. My future brother-in-law speculated correctly that "there must be a woman involved!

At church, Farrier had been asked to be part of a quartet, singing mostly tenor. The alto in the quartet was a young x-ray technician named Joan Hiebel. Later, the organist-director invited Walt and Joan to a dinner party. Both expected there would be crowd of people from the choir at the party, but when they arrived, they found only the organist-director, his wife, and each other.

> The other two were playing match makers—and it worked! We met in September of 1957, were in engaged in August of 1958 and after I went off to school in California, I flew home in January of 1959 to be married between blizzards.

Farrier had applied to the University of Southern California music school, because one of the guys he met in the service said that was the school for choral music.

> That was what I was interested in. I had directed the men's group at Yale and thought that was what I really wanted to do. The best choral program on the West Coast at that time was at USC. I applied to get into USC at the beginning of 1958, was accepted and off I went.
>
> I was at USC for one year to pick up my BA in music and two years to get my master's, for a total of three years. The first year was in music education. It was not specifically for choral, because I had to take several instrument classes, and I was in the USC concert band—not the marching band, that was too rah-rah for me—but I was in the concert band. I was required to take violin and all different kinds of instruments. Our drum major for the concert band was Mitch Leigh, the guy who wrote the music for *Man of La Mancha*. He was a very good clarinetist and a real clown. He played an E-flat clarinet, the little one, a fourth higher than an ordinary B-flat clarinet, almost like a soprano clarinet, which is a good name for it.
>
> I was in an advanced theory class, only about sixteen people in there but a really good bunch. We had several people in the class with absolute pitch. Every one of them had a color association with each pitch, and they would argue over, say, the color of B-flat. Most of these students were younger than I, undergrads, and hadn't been through college yet, and they argued constantly over the color of this pitch or that. It was something they had developed in their own mind. If one heard a G, that was yellow, and if it was G-sharp, it was

yellow with a greenish tint, but another would say, "Oh, you have to be kidding. G is blue!" The odd thing is that the persistence of these kids was not great. We had four of them, and two or three dropped out at the end of the first semester and never came back. I don't know why. Maybe they weren't interested in the intellectual side of music. They had to pass an audition with their particular instrument to be accepted at USC, but apparently all they wanted to do was perform.

Someone told me that instead of going through a placement agency to get a teaching job, I could get one through direct mail, so I sent letters to a variety of places and I think I got three replies. The only job available was a school in the Midwest paying $3,000 to $4,000 per year. We couldn't live on that. Even one person couldn't live on that and we had our first child in 1962.

At that time, I worked for an insurance company writing computer programs, which I recognized from the get-go was something I could do for a living. To be hired, they gave us paper-and-pencil tests on general math, manipulation of symbols, logic—particularly logic—and figuring out story problems. I was very much into math, had taken calculus and all that stuff. Musicians usually have a flair for math, so I was accepted to work as a computer programmer trainee the year I got my masters. I worked in Los Angeles for a year writing computer programs because, I would tell people, "Joan and I are addicted to living indoors and eating food.

The computers were really primitive. I remember for one project they wanted all of the programs to be able to update and have a daily update of all of the policies the company sold. They wanted this computerized so that at any given time they would have an accurate listing. They designed this great program, but the computers were so slow they couldn't finish running the program. It took twenty-eight hours for the program to finish running and they could only run it on the weekends, but at least the information was all on the computer.

I got my master's degree in 1961 and still didn't have a conducting job, but in the fall of 1962, I was able to get a job as choral director at Texas Lutheran College in Seguin, Texas, east of San Antonio. Seguin was a very small town, maybe fifteen thousand people, half of those migrants who followed crops up to the Canadian border every year. They were only in town during Christmas.

The chair of the music department said he would have preferred to be an actor, but the wages wouldn't allow him to support a family. What he did do was to build a summer theatre in the neighboring town of New Braunfels populated by people of German descent. The phone book had two and a half pages of Schmidts but not one single Smith. For two summers, I served as the music director, making friends with a wealthy man who was an actor in the theatre. He had five furniture stores, but his business was all paper and pencil, and it was difficult for him to keep track of what was where. He had me write a computer program for him using the coding I learned in Los Angeles so he could go to the computer and find his inventory at any store.

The theatre programming was musical comedy rotating with straight dramas, two weeks each: when one cast was performing, the other was rehearsing. I considered it the McDonalds version of producing shows. We would take frozen hot dogs in the morning to the theatre, put them in the sun, and by lunch time, they were hot. It worked out just fine. We got the chance to do not only the musical comedies but also began an annual Christmas choral festival, and of course it was warm there, so the performance was outdoors. We got big bleachers up: a bleacher for sopranos, a bleacher for altos, and a bleacher for the guys.

We did that for two years using the Texas Lutheran band, but the college did not have an orchestra. I wanted an orchestra so I could arrange and we could perform works such as a Bach cantata. In Texas, I had to rent an orchestra from San Antonio if we wanted to do an opera. In 1967, after five years in Seguin, I was hired as choral director by a school that did have a good orchestra program, Willamette University in Salem.

I was at Willamette for eleven years, ending in 1979. During that time, I taught all choral conducting, elementary music theory, music education, and individual voice. I liked being choral director at Willamette, but the longer I was there, the more nervous I was becoming. It was a mental thing mostly. I was getting more and more uptight trying to do too much. I had the big choir, a glee club for kids who didn't make the choir, madrigal singers and I also had a class in voice with as many as ten students. The choirs would all perform every other week or so. It was stressful because I walked out on the stage and no one had music. I had a little list I kept in my pocket on a 3 x 5 card with all the pieces we were going to perform and the key signature. Much of the music was a capella and tour material; we would go on tour each year, one for the madrigal group and one for the concert choir. I was doing all these choirs every single year and until my last two years, I received no help.

The last year, I was made chair of the music department and that was not for me. I had a fight with them to give me an extra $1,000 a year for being chair. As it was, when I worked for them, they routinely paid all the music people 10 percent less than pay for other fields. The president of the college made no bones about it; I talked to him face to face and he said, "We don't need to pay musicians as much because of supply and demand. We pay you people 10 percent less than the rest of the faculty, and we will do fine." Earlier in 1971, Joan hurt her knee, requiring nine operations, the last of which was a knee replacement. The state would help out with the medical finances if I could prove my salary was low enough. When Joan showed them my contract, they looked at it, pulled open a little book and said, "If you had a third child, you would be eligible for food stamps." That really hit me. In the spring of 1978, I wondered did I really want to do this? Here I was working myself to death. We already had two children, and now if we had one child more, we would be on food stamps. By that time, our oldest son was only a year away from college. I thought, *This isn't going to work.*

Farrier started working for the state of Oregon in 1979, writing computer programs.

I worked for them for eighteen and a half years, retiring in March of 1997. My work at the state was not even close to being as fulfilling as a choral director. However, as a computer programmer, bottom level, working for the state here in Salem, which is not a high paying outfit for computer people, my first paycheck was within a dollar of what I had made as a faculty member at Willamette with a master's degree, tenure, and sixteen years of experience. The state had a much better health program; Public Employees Retirement System (PERS) was a far better deal financially. Part of the strain of working at Willamette was the low pay

> and benefits. Without our church money, we would never have been able to manage it.

All along, Farrier was being paid as a singer at St. Paul's Episcopal Church.

> I had started doing that soon after we arrived in Salem. Joan started there immediately; she was hired as a soloist before the summer was over in September of 1967 when we were still living in a motel. We moved into our present house on Oct. 3, 1967, and have been in that house now for more than fifty-one years. The organist at St. Paul's Church later recruited Joan to be in the church symphonic choir. A tenor, who was a lawyer, quit at St. Paul's in January, and I started in February of 1968. We were desperately poor, because we didn't even have enough money to get our stuff back from the moving company. We finally had to borrow money from the Marion-Polk teachers credit union.

Much of what Farrier has done after retiring from the state is in connection with the St. Paul's Episcopal Church. He had been a paid soloist for twenty-seven years. "Two years ago, St. Paul's went from two services—which they had forever—to only one service at 10:00 a.m. Like most churches nationwide, the membership had sagged."

Farrier has worked extensively with Paul Klemme (the music pastor) at St. Paul's. Klemme is employed at the church but also at Willamette University: full time at the church and part time at Willamette.

> Paul Klemme is doing everything in the world. He does the men's choir at Willamette, he teaches organ at Willamette, and he is doing our choir. Because he is a crackerjack organist, he does guest shots. When people have a tough organ part, they will call him up for this group or that group, something in Portland several times a year. He also runs the Willamette Master Chorus. Willamette University makes Hudson Hall available for the chorus to have rehearsals and performances.

The only thing Farrier got paid for at St. Paul's was being a tenor soloist, but he built stage sets for Klemme. He built the entire set for

Amahl and the Night Visitors. When he purchased a computer in 1991, he started doing inclusions, printing out music for the church bulletin, but mainly what he has done for Klemme is music arrangements.

> I am sort of Paul's right-hand man. He likes to bring brass groups in; Paul himself used to be a brass player. He hires brass groups and good ones like Brett Randolph. He gets the top people in the area, and so he always needs arrangements. Frequently he will, say, switch to having two trombones instead of three trombones, so I need to readjust this arrangement for different voices. I have to revise the arrangements. I orchestrate and then play that back for him. My software will play back one, two, or three trumpets. It plays all the instruments at once, which is great because you can hear the things that don't work before the first rehearsal. You don't have to go back and say "that didn't work." Until I got the computer, I had to hear all the parts in my head. That is what everyone had to do before they had computers, but it is a lot easier with one.

Farrier does most of his arranging for Advent, the season leading up to Christmas.

> It starts about five weeks before Christmas. It is the coming, the entrance to—the general idea is that the Savior is coming. I did a whole series of arrangements for voices and instruments and we did an entire evening of that. In this case, I did both compositions and arrangements. The entire concert was material I had either composed or arranged, arrangements for brass groups and for flute groups.
>
> I have orchestrated for a full orchestra. My biggest orchestration was for Kitty McKinnon's (a former piano teacher in Salem) piece, *Noah's Scrapbook*, a forty-five-minute work. She composed it for piano and vocalist, and it was performed for the first time not too long after we came to Salem, about 1969, and it has been performed several times, twice at St. Paul's. The year before, St. Paul's had an entire evening of Kitty's compositions. Kitty and I decided it would be great to do that for a full orchestra (still including a vocalist), the kind of chamber orchestra used for the annual concert at the Kroc Center, a kids-getting-in-free concert. It had been a wonderful thing that unfortunately died when the

> chamber orchestra died. It was a concert that kids would like, which included well-known pieces such as *Tubby the Tuba*, *Peter and the Wolf*, and *A Young Person's Guide to the Orchestra*.
>
> I orchestrated most of *Noah's Scrapbook* just as Kitty's health was getting worse and worse. We had been working two to three afternoons a week on the piece for a year, and Kitty still wanted to make some changes. We had 85 percent of it orchestrated when on a Thursday morning in November, she was taken to urgent rehab just west of Portland. She didn't have a chance to see the newspaper headlines, and thank heavens, because the headline that same morning said "Salem Chamber Orchestra Declares Bankruptcy." She never saw the headline; her son, Scott, made sure she never saw it. We went up to see her the following Sunday—she seemed to be not in terrible shape—and of course, up there no one told her. She died on the following Tuesday. It was remarkably quick; no one expected it to be that quick. She never did know that her piece was not going to be used at the Kroc Center. I had even talked with the director of the Salem Chamber Orchestra, Nikolas Caoile (pronounced Kawee'le). He was very much interested in doing that, because there had been only three pieces that really worked for a children's audience, the three that I mentioned. Kitty's piece would have been a great addition. It was set to ten funny poems about animals. It was never performed anywhere. I could still finish it, but who is going to perform it? It now would last about forty-eight minutes.

Having his full symphony orchestration performed may be the one accomplishment that has eluded Walt Farrier. He helped form a stage band in junior high, played in elite bands, sang as a soloist and in choir, directed a choir, helped form a new choir, taught voice lessons and theory, was music department chair at a college, and has written untold compositions, arrangements, and orchestrations. If Farrier cannot be considered a Renaissance man in music, I am unable to say who can.

Randy Kem

Randy Kem will tell you the music retail business has changed dramatically since he began working for Wills Music in 1977. In those days, customers would come in and buy a brand new trombone. They might have shopped different stores for pricing, but in the end, they made an in-store purchase. Of course, many parents rented instruments for their kids, but the purchase of new and used instruments was still a significant percentage of sales. Now nearly all of that has vanished.

In partnership with three others, Kem has his own store called Willamette Valley Music Company and is doing well but not because of retail sales. He laments that people are buying musical instruments almost exclusively online. He said,

> Retail prices made it possible for people working in a store to have a family. The store generated enough money to pay for insurance and retirement. Now potential "customers" will stand in the store, look at something, take a photo, and then get on their phones to search out internet retailers and find out how prices compare.
>
> At first, many of the manufacturers resisted the temptation to sell directly to the consumer, but now even some of the American-known names, some of the big ones like Fender guitar, have a direct portal.
>
> EBay is a big factor in used instruments—people look at that site and can find an instrument for a much lower price. There are many of us who feel that eBay is the world's biggest fence, the easiest, most accessible way to sell stolen property. Why? Because I can sell anonymously. If I steal someone's saxophone here in Salem and try to sell it on Craigslist or to the school, it

is tracked. The serial number is easily traceable. But if I steal the sax and try to sell it to someone in Vermont, I can do it. eBay does not require serial numbers and doesn't make me do what the state of Oregon makes pawnshops do. Pawnshops have to hold the instrument for thirty days and check with the state to make sure it is not listed as being stolen. On eBay, I don't have to do that. People also buy directly from overseas. The Chinese equivalent of eBay is Alibaba.

The shift has forced us from a sales industry to a service industry. We still rent instruments because the online rental option—even though many companies are trying to do it—still isn't an effective way to reach families. Our rental programs are strong and our repair service is still strong. Sending an instrument off to a central repair service in Indiana from Oregon is not an efficient way to get a child's instrument repaired. Retail music is therefore a service industry and it is piecework, whether renting an instrument or repair work. That has been our focus. We still have pianos, other instruments, and sheet music for sale, but the driving force is our service industry.

Kem has spent nearly his entire life in western Oregon. As a performer, he has played all over from Vancouver, British Columbia, to New York and California, but he has always liked Salem. He sees it as a good place to raise children, have community ties, and have the opportunity to stay employed.

He spent all his school years in north Salem. One of his band teachers was Russ Whitmer at Hoover Elementary. Whitmer had been a long-time band director at North High, but by the time Kem came along, he was doing only elementary schools. Grant Hagestedt was his junior high band director at Waldo Junior High and Del Chinburg his high school director. Chinburg came from Wyoming and took over the high school job when Whitmer went to the elementary. Kem went to Oregon College of Education (now Western Oregon University) for two and a half years and Willamette for one year. He was intending all along to be a music teacher. He had enough experience as a professional musician playing the saxophone (and sometimes clarinet and flute) and, with the travel involved, knew that life wasn't for him.

He decided to work for Wills Music in 1977 when Vern Wiscarson owned the store. It was still on State Street when Kem arrived, but he became involved in helping move the store to its final Court Street location. Not long after, Edna Wiscarson—now a widow—sold the store, and it was never what it once was. Kem was still there but supplemented his income by playing casual gigs with Martin Behnke, the new band director at Willamette University. Behnke talked Kem into teaching and made arrangements for him to go back to school at Willamette. Kem did some student teaching and realized teaching—like being a professional musician—wasn't going to be his future career.

Kem decided to get out of the music business altogether and ran restaurants—he was a manager at Spaghetti Warehouse and the Union Oyster Bar for a number of years in the early 1980s. By this time, he was married and had two sons. He continued with the restaurant business, but one day he took a job with a big band traveling for a job on the coast. On the way, he shared a back seat with Fran Allen, who was the long-time repairman for Weathers Music Store. As they talked, Allen agreed to take Kem on as an apprentice to learn band instrument repair. Kem spent one-and-a-half years learning the craft, and became the man doing all the repairs for Keith Weathers from 1987 until the store closed in 2012. Kem was an independent contractor with a handshake agreement from Weathers all those years.

When Weathers told Kem he was going to retire, the two tried to work out an arrangement for Kem to purchase the store, but the store was too big, much of it in retail inventory, and Kem was not in a position to buy a business that would ever benefit him and his new partners: Mike Delamare, his son Eli Kem and Eli's wife Kathryn Kem. He opened Willamette Valley Music November 11, 2011. Weathers didn't close his store until the next year, but both knew it was coming, and Kem was able to help with the transition.

Today, Willamette Valley Music has become firmly established in rental and repair, 80 to 90 percent of that business coming from music education. Kem said,

> We are totally focused on servicing the schools. We have active repair and sales accounts with every middle school and high school in Salem, and we do a number of things with the elementary schools too. We also deal with many outlying schools in the Willamette Valley and at least seven schools down in southern Oregon.

Of all the business coming from schools, at least half of that is Salem-Keizer. Salem-Keizer has eleven middle schools plus Howard Street Charter School and six high schools. Most of the middle schools have a connection with the elementary school beginning band and orchestra. Kem said,

> The classroom teachers in all those elementary schools have budgets with different needs, and we see a little of that money but not much. We don't do much with the choral people; most of their purchasing is sheet music, all done online.
>
> For schools, it is legally complicated to rent instruments, so I work directly with the families. The band and orchestra teachers will gather information from the music stores in the area and pass that out to families on family conference nights. Hopefully all these folks will go out and rent an instrument for their kids to start the band program, but the rent rates have not matched inflation. If you were renting a flute for fourteen to fifteen dollars per month in the 1970s, now it is 2015, and we rent flutes for only twenty to twenty-five per month. The school district, of course, supplies many instruments to families with limited incomes. These families are identified in ways such as their kids qualified for free breakfast and lunch. These instruments are available to these kids if they participate in band and orchestra.
>
> We think of the primary instruments in band as being the clarinet, flute, trumpet, and trombone. Some of the teachers will allow the kids to start on saxophone or percussion, but basic band consists of those four instruments. Those four are the biggest block of instruments that we rent for band. For strings,

the violins, violas, cellos, and basses are sized, anything from a 1/16th to a full size. By far most of our business is connecting with directors, who in turn connect with families.

We do a large amount of instrument repair for schools but some much more than others. Money, for the thirty-five years I have been here, has always been allotted to schools in a disproportionate way. All schools receive money from the general fund in the same way, but music teachers in a certain building will be told they must use all their budget money by February, and no more money for the rest of the year. After February, they can't get instruments repaired; they can't buy anything. Other schools come to the end of the year in June with $5,000 set aside, and the teachers can get all needed repairs done. We can take care of that, and they don't have to spend any of next year's money. How did one school collect $5,000 for the band program at the end of the year, but the other school ran out of money in February? The first school is not a wealthier school; this is money from the general fund. It is true that some schools have to pay more for remedial education, but that should be offset by extra money from the state and federal government. If the school has a child with a disability in a wheelchair, someone must be with him full time, and there should be money for that, but maybe these costs are not 100 percent covered. Teachers and administrators are forced into additional bookkeeping to track every student in the school. They aren't just tracking academically but also for family needs, discipline, and extracurricular activities, because if there is money available, then the school has to make applications for that money to be spent.

The Recession put a big dent in our business, because the schools cut back severely in different areas. For one year in 1983, when we had that economic slowdown, the Salem-Keizer School District completely eliminated band in the elementary schools. By not having band for one year, those kids had to wait until the sixth grade to start, and I watched that cycle of less quality all the way through the students' senior year. I remember going through the process of getting beginning band reinstated; it took us a while to get the numbers back to where they once were. The sixth grade band was smaller, then seventh grade, and on up through high school. Without that steady motion through the system, music education suffered. It definitely affected Keith

Weathers that one year. He had already purchased instruments and accessories and unexpectedly did not rent the number of instruments he thought he would, but he still had to pay for them. If the store buys fifty saxophones but only rents ten, the manufacturers still expect him to pay for the other forty.

The manufacturers also took a hit during the Great Recession. They were buying raw materials, but in a sense, they were playing with a crystal ball, because what will five years from now look like? They have to buy the raw materials, it has to be shipped, they can't wait until March and say, "This is what will happen in the fall.

The school's fiscal system runs for two years, but it also has a ten-year plan, an eight-year plan, and a six-year plan in addition to the two years. They track births, watch what the builders are doing, how renters are doing, populations moving in and out. There can be a bubble on home buying, and if there are more homes sold under a certain amount of money, that means more new families in the area. If the percentage of homes are more expensive, there will be less young kids. New families are not going to afford expensive houses.

When Dallas (Oregon) dumped the music program completely during the Recession, it wasn't totally a fiscal choice. The folks there thought the music program was costing more than the district was gaining in benefits. They panicked about their graduation rates and literacy requirements. Their solution was to bring more teachers in for remedial work, and to do that, they had to sacrifice arts.

If Salem had gone the way of Dallas, would it have been worth my time and the time of Mike, Eli, and Kathy to be in the position of being all in? Everything that we had was going into this business. Would it have been worth the risk? Conceptually, the business is worth the risk. It is fun, it is exhausting, everyone is working six to seven days a week, often working evenings driving to Ashland and Klamath Falls to make the business work. I love that part of it, but I am at a point where my kids are grown. My sense of risk is different than it was when I was young and had a family. Am I going to sacrifice all this and, if it goes sideways, start over? In ten years, if it goes south, I get to retire.

Should we take the risk and go the way of some stores in California? When Proposition 13 came to California, some of the school music programs there closed. The stores started their own music programs and made agreements with local schools, which allowed them to use space where the kids were. The music stores hired the music teachers, brought in the instruments, and kept programs going, and they did that all over California in different ways in different communities. But there had to be community involvement and schools that were willing to lease the music section of the building for after school and a music store that would take that on. Music is an organizational structure that is huge, and it placed all the financial burden on the families. The store owners had to figure out how to rent instruments at a price per month that not only paid for the instrument but for the instruction and the facility. Even if the schools were willing to let the store use the cafeteria after school, someone still had to pay for the insurance. At some point, someone has to pony up for whatever is needed. Stores are still doing that down in California and are becoming nonprofits, because eventually, if they have enough activity going and enough money is coming through the store in terms of a retail application, the store has to pay taxes on it. If it becomes a nonprofit, as long as the store is not making a profit, no one is paying taxes except for the employees who are paying their own personal taxes. Teachers are getting a decent salary, but they aren't getting the benefits they had as a public school teacher from the city, county, the state, and the federal government. The teachers working in California are independent contractors. They are just getting money and have to figure out their own benefits. All this manages to keep some stores alive, but many of them have disappeared.

In Salem, the schools have developed a special relationship with the community. Our property taxes aren't what they could be, because so much of our downtown property is all government owned in one way or another. The county doesn't pay taxes, the state doesn't pay taxes, the federal government doesn't pay taxes, the city of Salem doesn't pay taxes, nor do the schools and churches. Instead, all the onus is on business owners and personal property taxes. In Salem, we are much different than many communities

> because of the large infrastructure of government properties. You have to admire how fiscally responsible we are in Salem. I'm sure we could find waste in every school, but overall, given what they do to keep the programs here at such a high level, it is really amazing. In Salem, they do an area of budgeting; each school is given money for certain things, and it has to be spent that way. Each school also gets a large pool of money through the district general fund, and the school decides where the money goes. The building principal, after paying salaries, gets to make those choices individually.

Along with teachers and administrators, people like Kem are trying to create future music parents and listeners. He said,

> The music program helped me in school whether it was being with my friends or keeping me interested in school on days when I was discouraged. Hopefully, when parents start a family, they will have their kids involved in music. The kids will play or listen to a concert instead of staying home and doing something else. It is good for young people to be engaged and to go out and listen.

Nicole Elwell, Lindsey Elwell Gellenbeck, and Jennifer Lewis

In January of 2016, I received a call from McNary High School asking if I could do an emergency piano tuning. Unlike the norm, the caller was not a music teacher or someone from the front office but a student: a teenage girl. She was calling in behalf of Jim Taylor, the choir teacher. As I noted in the Jim Taylor bio, he gave students loads of responsibility. This included making phone calls and setting up appointments.

Taylor said that most of the students who were his office help were not choir kids but those taking business classes. Nicole Elwell, Lindsey Elwell Gellenbeck, and Jennifer Lewis were exceptions. They were musical *and* organization/business types. They were among a string—about four at a time—who "ran" the choir and did all the logistical minutiae that made Taylor's life much easier. As he will testify, these three young women and others did a superb job of keeping things in order while he was there. Like Cheyenne Hayes at Sprague, their experience in high school was a springboard for greater things to come.

The girls were not necessarily contemporaries at McNary, at least not Nicole Elwell. She graduated in 2009, three years before her sister, Lindsey, and four years before Jennifer Lewis. During her freshman year, McNary lost its choir director in the middle of the year, and Taylor arrived as a replacement. When Elwell told her mother, Julie Smith Elwell, about the new choir director, she discovered that Taylor had been good friends with her mother's family;

her mom had sung in choir with Taylor at Sprague High School. Taylor's brother was Elwell's uncle's best friend. Elwell started giving Taylor hints that she knew of his family and the mutual friendships, and from that connection, she ended up becoming his aide during one of her free periods.

Taylor did not teach choir during that period. Elwell and another girl would sit down with Taylor and brainstorm where they wanted the choir to go for the next tour. Elwell said,

"He told us, 'All right, you guys are in charge of a tour to San Francisco. Look into how much hotels are going to cost, where we want to go, and all that sort of thing,' so I spent time researching everything and how to put it together." Elwell called different charter bus companies, told them how many kids were going, how long they would be gone, and so forth. She narrowed it down by price and found the transportation company the choir used. The same was true for hotels: she was not used to booking for 100 students and trying to get a group rate for fifty rooms. She said the hotels were willing to work with her, not just the hotel in San Francisco but hotels coming and going. When planning the tour, she had no help. She worked up the itinerary, hotels, transportation, restaurants, sightseeing, going to a performance—everything. She made a travel book that told kids and parents the top places to go. She organized kids into groups, each group governed by a chaperone. If a student didn't want to go to a certain tourist attraction, he or she was to link up with another group. She organized all that before the kids left on the tour.

Elwell made the flyers and wrote the emails that Taylor sent to the parents, asking for chaperones and other necessities. She wondered if it wouldn't have been easier to go to New York, Disneyland, or Hawaii. She said, "There is more publicity for those kinds of places; I might have done a little less research. I felt if I had started from the very beginning, I definitely could have planned a larger trip."

There is one part of the tour Elwell did not plan. Taylor set up choir clinics all along the tour. He was the one who had the relationships with the various choir teachers and professors, but Elwell was given the assignment to look up the various directors and get their phone numbers. Her sister, Lindsey Elwell Gellenbeck, said,

> Mr. Taylor was ultimately responsible and the overall leader of the trip. Nothing major went wrong. Some things might not have gone super smoothly, but I can't remember them. He ran a tight ship; the kids respected him and looked up to him. There was no misbehaving or anything like that. The kids knew when it was time to have fun and when it was time to step up and work. He was good at holding the tour to the itinerary, and he relied on parents. He was good at doing that.

One of the clinics Taylor set up was with the choir director at Southern Oregon University in Ashland. Lindsey remembered that clinic to be one of the best experiences she had on the tour. I keep mentioning Lindsey in the goings-on of the tour because Nicole planned the tour and then graduated. She missed the trip, but Lindsey was the beneficiary of Nicole's planning and had all the fun.

Lindsey was three years younger than Nicole, graduating from McNary in 2012. She followed in her sister's footsteps to some degree. She assumed office duties, became the manager and, along with Jennifer Lewis, did all the organizing and communicating for Taylor for choir activities. Lindsey said, "Jennifer and I became his right-hand girls. He depended on us for everything." What Lindsey will be remembered for is teaching at-risk kids in Taylor's piano lab program. As Taylor has said, hundreds of kids went through the program when Lindsey was there.

Jennifer Lewis graduated from McNary in 2013. She did not consider herself specifically a business student but an all-around student and, like the Elwell sisters, was always involved with choir. Like the Elwells, she became a valuable aide. It was said that when Taylor gave Lewis an assignment, he never had to worry about it. During a rehearsal, Taylor might call her out and say, "This is what we need to do here." Each assignment was an increase in her leadership ability. When Taylor was out sick, Lewis worked with other student leaders to make sure the rehearsals ran smoothly.

Lewis was not so much involved with tours but played a major role in planning and facilitating events. She helped run the monthly coffee shop concerts and the annual Night of Hope benefit concert at the Liberty House Women's Crisis Center. When she and others planned a small concert, they had to decide what music would be performed, initiate auditions, acquire microphones and other sound equipment, oversee proper lighting and other features for ambiance, set up chairs and seating, make refreshments available for patrons, and take care of the clean up afterward. Extensive coordination was necessary, and these events were completely student run. The kids went to local businesses to ask if they were willing to donate certain items or sell them at a lower cost. They worked with Uptown Music for spotlights and other equipment for the evening.

When Lewis was with the jazz choir, she helped run Valegrams—a fundraiser in which she and others provided a song that others paid for to serenade an individual. The guys sang to girls, girls sang to the guys, and the entire choir drove around the community to croon to people at other schools the day before Valentine's Day and at McNary on the day itself.

One huge event Lewis was connected with was Knight of Arts held yearly at McNary. She was doing what other people weren't doing and running around asking where she could be helpful. She worked with the choir rehearsals, with the costume people, technology experts, and in the general planning of the evening. Lewis said the adults ran Knight of Arts, but the students helped make it work. She was detail oriented, which made her a valuable asset for the evening.

She tried to run the choir office with greater capacity, providing general leadership, and the things she did in high school helped prepare her for life in college. She said,

> I was forced to take on a new level of leadership throughout the choir program, and that experience helped me be the person I am today. I am able to identify areas of need and take charge. Once you have helped run a program, it is much easier to run the next one, to take that experience and translate it to others.

Lewis had just graduated from Pacific Lutheran University when I spoke with her. In addition to studying marketing and resource management, she was the student chapter club president for Human Resource Management (SHRM or Society for Human Resource Management). She was an orientation guide for new students for four years in a row and was club president for a group called Ignite, a Christian ministry group on campus. In connection with her church, she was a worship leader and Bible study leader.

Lewis's main focus now is her parent's companies: Lewis Designs (web development) and Salem Aerial (involving aerial drone photography). She said she gets to work on the creative as well as the technical side and is heavily involved with marketing, meeting potential clients along with her parents. She has her own business that is small right now: freelance calligraphy with brush pens. She is preparing herself for a greater administrative role in her church, and she sings and writes her own music, most of it worship related. All this she considers a fun experience she wouldn't have had if she had not been in choir for nine years.

Lindsey Elwell Gellenbeck married and is a stay-at-home-mom. In addition to being busy with her young children, she teaches piano lessons to a growing number of students. She was considered a superb pianist at McNary. She said,

> One thing that has transferred from choir into my adult life is that Mr. Taylor treated all of us, especially the leaders, like adults, and he expected us to act that way. It gave the leaders confidence to fulfill roles that were above what a high school student is normally given, to being expected to act like an adult, take on the responsibility, and follow through with it.

Nicole Elwell received her bachelor of science in nursing. Her specialty for nine years had been providing rehab for patients (mainly the elderly) between hospital and home. She said,

> It means a lot to these folks to have someone visit them. To be a high school student and plan a tour for kids gave me the oppor-

> tunity at a young age to step into a role of leadership and responsibility, and now I have to do the same thing in nursing. I am responsible for my floor. I have people under me, and ultimately I am responsible for the patients. I have learned to organize and be a leader by example without being overbearing.

At the time I spoke with Nicole, she was about to travel to be a nurse in Nairobi, Kenya. She said,

> When you go to Africa, there is a language barrier, but when we listen to music or sing together, we can sing the same song in different languages and have a deep connection. Lindsey and I are both heavily involved in music. We still sing at church. Lindsey teaches piano, I play the piano some, and we both have the possibility to change people's lives.

Steve Phillips

I met Steve Phillips back in the 1980s when he was still at Sprague High School and a classmate of my two sons. He must have been at our home, but most likely I saw him performing with the Sprague Concert Choir. He was memorable in his own way: friendly but quiet and respectful, never boisterous. Other than choir, I had no idea of what his interests were. I didn't know his connection to music was anything more than superficial.

Fast forward more than two decades to the District Choir Festival held at Western Oregon University. When I walked into the lobby of the Leonard W. Rice Auditorium, there was Phillips sitting behind a table representing the Oregon Music Educators Association (OMEA), which sponsors the event. I recognized him instantly as he did me. He was friendly and gracious as ever. Traffic was light, so we had a chance for a mad quick exchange of our lives. (I saw him the following year sitting behind the same table when the District Festival was again held in Monmouth.)

He told me I should visit Auburn Elementary in a few days; his second graders were putting on a concert. I accepted the invitation and arrived at 5:30 p.m. The theme was "It Sounds a Little Fishy to Me" with songs devoted to—you guessed it—ichthyology. It was a fun, well organized evening with plenty of teachers along with kids participating.

Phillips is unusual in that he has been the general music teacher at Auburn Elementary in east Salem for more than twenty years. Some of his kids are children of parents he taught a generation before. He can teach at one location because with more than seven hundred children, Auburn is one of the largest elementary schools in Salem-Keizer.

He teaches twenty general music classes every week, kindergarten through fifth grade, plus choir twice a week. Auburn is large enough that two other teachers come in to teach the remaining seven general music classes. Auburn sits in a lower-middle-class area with hordes of kids living in apartments, many of them with single parents. The school is Title 1 with 100 percent of kids on free and reduced lunch. Despite the demographic, Phillips is grateful for the tremendous support from the Auburn Parent Club. He said, "They support everything at school, not just music."

Phillips developed a strong interest in music education from experiences with middle school and high school choir teachers, Debra Klatz and Gary Frame. Through Frame, he met Karl Raschkes, the music supervisor. He said,

> I think Karl had a lot of confidence in me. I grew up going to Sprague and graduating with Ted Raschkes, who was Karl's son. Karl did a musical analysis of a piece I wrote and sang at our high school graduation. I still have the piece and the concentrated, interesting analysis he wrote.

Phillips graduated from Western Oregon University in music education. When he graduated, he interviewed with Raschkes for a position in the Salem-Keizer School District but was turned down. "Karl said at the time, 'This is not the right market for hiring. The music staff is pretty set, but I want to get you in the district. Come see me in a couple of years.'"

Phillips found a job as a choral director in the Philomath School District, teaching at Philomath Middle School and in outlying schools such as Blodgett and Kings Valley. In 1996, he received notice that the elementary music program in Philomath was being removed because of tax cuts. He came back to see Raschkes for a position in Salem-Keizer, and this time he was hired to teach at Auburn Elementary where he still is today. After he was hired in Salem, Philomath called and said the district had more money and was going to bring back the choral program. "Will you stay?" they asked. Phillips said, "Sorry."

When Phillips interviewed in Salem, Auburn and Gubser Elementary were open for new music teachers. The principals from both schools were in the room, accompanied by Raschkes. That evening, Phillips got a call from human resources and was offered a job at Auburn. He said,

> Salem-Keizer is known for its turnaround, for letting people know quickly. The interviews were that day and done, and I heard that night. I have seen districts where they interview, and you can find out a week or two later. That entire time I am going (he draws in a deep breath), "Did I? Did I not??"

After teaching for so many years, Phillips has found himself on the other side of the interview process. He was on interview teams with Raschkes right before he retired. He said,

> It is an amazing experience. I have been on teams with Mary Lou Boderman (the present music supervisor) as well. Mary Lou is wonderful. In elementary, the candidates have to show musician skills, sing intervals, conduct. That is the first part of the interview. During the interview, I ask questions also. I ask them to sing. I ask musical questions such as giving us their philosophy on different musical ideologies and theories. Mary Lou or Karl have drawn up the questions beforehand. I will read the questions that are prepared. I may need to ask or answer follow-up questions. Now I have been on an interview team at least five times. They rotate it around; it is a great experience; I really enjoy doing it. It is like a rite of passage when we interview these young kids right out of college. They have wanted to be a music teacher and they go through that same process I went through. The applicants are not always just out of college; sometimes we get folks from other districts who have ten years of experience, but there always seems to be a Salem rite of passage, especially if they are going for an elementary position.

In general music at Auburn, Phillips incorporates the two main styles of teaching: Kodaly (pronounced Ko-dai') and Orff. He said,

> If you are a strong teacher, you want to have a bit of both and making the two mesh. The Kodaly method is very much a singing approach system using solfège hand signals. It uses rote; rote is a strong part of the Kodaly philosophy. Orff is a method using musical instruments, but teachers can through Orff use instruments that lead into singing, imagination, and musical play. This is all general music. I want to have different strategies, different ideologies of thinking. I use both methods for all ages of kids.

From the beginning, Phillips had to adapt to teaching age groups from kindergarten through fifth grade.

> When I was a first-year teacher, one of the smartest things I ever did was to develop a curriculum roadmap that says when kids comes to kindergarten, these are the skills I want them to know. I then know that when they are hitting first grade, they can do x. At the end of the first grade, here is what I want them to know and on and on through the fifth grade. I lay out the skills I want the kids to know when they leave Auburn, and I am working with them to reach those skills.

Phillips was the perfect person to help develop the district's elementary Scope and Sequence (Salem-Keizer's standard for what students should know at a certain stage in musical education). There had been a Scope and Sequence at the secondary level, but over a period of years, Phillips and others developed a Scope and Sequence for the elementary level and made district standards align with national standards even though the national plan was considered broad and vague. He said,

> We have to separate the national standards from the district standards. Ten years ago, elementary music was thought of by many as fluff. The kids would come in and play; there wasn't any focus, no theory. The school principals understood that. Other teachers thought that and there wasn't a real perception of drive to elementary music instruction. I was on the first committee in the school district to change that. We developed our own Scope and Sequence, because I am one who wanted that drive. I said,

There has to be theory. If we are leading these kids toward the promised land in high school, they have to have a theoretical background before they ever get there." I have always been theory based. There were teachers teaching theory before and some who were not. The prevailing sentiment was if some people teach theory—good. If some don't—oh well, so these school principals had good reason to feel that way.

In the last ten years, elementary music teachers have gradually made theory central to teaching. Before that, theory wasn't taught until middle school. Debra Klatz at Judson Middle School thought it was important to make theory the backbone of her teaching. When we were in Gary Frame's choirs at Sprague High, he thought it was important to teach theory behind the music we were singing, but Debra instilled that theory mindset, preparing us for Gary's choirs. In the last ten years, elementary music teachers have accepted the challenge and are motivated to teach theory. When kids get to middle school, there is a continuum of theory that stays on through high school.

No matter what method I use, some kids will always be more advanced than others. If I have kids who have had piano lessons, I am constantly developing enrichment activities in a way for these kids to assist others who don't have those skills. What is that rhythm? Hey, here is what he is talking about. The piano students provide assistance and enrichment for struggling kids to gain learning and structure. There are different ways to approach challenges, of getting all kids on course. I had a fifth grader who acquired the most incredible grasp of theory of any kid I ever had. I developed activities for him to apply what he knew. Now he is playing for the youth symphony and is part of his own family band. His parents are very musical, very big supporters of me, just terrific people.

I also receive solid support from the middle school teachers in this area, which makes a great difference. I am grateful to Rita Brown, orchestra teacher, Ryan Udall, band teacher, and Mary Brandenstein, choral director. They do great work.

I have had a variety of principals over the years, some who have a strong musical background themselves and are very supportive, but some principals who don't have that background consider music an "activity" much like recess. For those people,

I try to encourage them and give them that musical background. When a new principal comes in, I sit down with him or her as soon as possible to orient, to say "here is my philosophy" and that approach is probably encouraged throughout the district. I show the importance of what I do, show the research, and the new principal is almost always on board. In this I go further than many teachers. Being in this district for twenty years now, I have seen the value and research and try to get administrators to see that value. I have those conversations with them and invite them to class. If they can see what the kids are doing, that they are talking about me, the parents are talking about me, and if that is happening, the administrators will also be talking about me. I am one of the more visible people at the school.

Is Salem-Keizer School District a magnet? Absolutely. Because of the stability, the support, the reputation of the program, when I am teaching in Salem-Keizer, there is a feeling of being in the strongest district in the state. I feel that. The secondary teachers absolutely care about what I do. This is amazing because I know all the music teachers in Salem-Keizer, especially those that feed into North High School. We in the North area know the goal, the mecca the kids are heading toward. We know that what we are doing and what we are preparing will ultimately lead them to success at North High School.

Marti Bowles

Over the years, a music therapist at the Oregon State Hospital would call and ask me to tune one of the pianos on campus. She would lead me to where the piano was located, and that was the association in summa. Thus I have never understood what a music therapist actually does. Until I met Marti Bowles.

Bowles was working at the state hospital in Salem when I spoke with her but she hails from Utah and recently went back there to work.

Marti has always associated with music in some way. She took up the cello in the fifth grade and continued to play it through high school. In middle school, she had exceptional teachers who challenged her. One in particular stood out and got more out of her than her private instructors.

But her main instrument was piano. She began taking lessons when she was four years old, and by high school, she was playing for the jazz band. When it was time to go to college, she wanted to major in piano performance. She sent out audition tapes and auditioned in person.

One of the auditions was at Utah State University in Logan. When Bowles arrived, she discovered there were also auditions for the music therapy program. She had heard about music therapy and figured she might as well audition for that as well. What was there to lose, she thought. By that time, music therapy programs were becoming competitive. Of the fifty people who auditioned every year, Utah State took fifteen or twenty. She passed the audition.

Bowles leaned toward music therapy because she had an interest in mental health. She noticed that at Utah State, many of the classes were the same as those in music education. She took classes in music history, analysis training, aural skills training, and theory, especially advanced theory. She had been in an advanced placement theory class in high school and loved it. During her coursework in music theory, she was exposed to all kinds of settings including special ed at a nursing home and working with inmates at the Cache County jail, learning what the environment was like. The experience increased her interest in mental health.

Bowles finished her course work in 2013, but in order to graduate, she had to do an internship. She checked with the national organization for music therapy to see what internships were possible around the country with specific training in mental health. She connected with a music therapist at the conference who informed her that there was an internship opening in Salem, Oregon, and that the work was in one of the most innovative psychiatric forensic hospitals in the nation. This was the hospital from which other hospitals drew ideas.

When her internship was over, her supervisors considered her successful enough to offer her a position in the state hospital.

The Oregon State Hospital had gone through a huge change from the time *One Flew Over the Cuckoo's Nest* was filmed there in 1975. The buildings on both sides of Center Street were outdated and in need of replacement. This replacement was completed in 2012; all buildings on the north side were abandoned and slated for demolition. The buildings on the south side were gutted or upgraded. Now with modern buildings, the campus has a cheery feel, and the buildings have names instead of numbers.

There are three categories of patients at the hospital. One concerns those who have been civilly committed and are not involved with the corrections system (they have not committed a crime but are in the hospital because of the potential danger they can impose on themselves or others). They have been committed by a guardian, or they are not doing well in a group home. They stay at the hospital until they are ready to go back to the community.

At the other end of the spectrum are those who have been found not guilty by reason of insanity. They are at the hospital as a result of a plea option; they admit that they committed a crime, but it was done because of mental illness. The court has decided they didn't know what they were doing and couldn't control their actions. While at the hospital, they are under a review board that determines when they can leave the hospital and transition back into the community. They do not go back to prison and are not subject to a conviction. It is all part of the plea option, but if they leave the hospital, they are still subject to a review board and a continuation of their charges.

Bowles works with a middle category of patients who are caught between the mental health system and the legal system. They have been arrested and charged with a crime, but they can't move forward with a court case because their mental illness impacts their ability to understand what is going on, to make choices, to work with their attorney, and to make sure their symptoms aren't getting in the way of their progress. As a group, they are called "unable to aid and assist." They are court ordered to the hospital in the middle of their court proceedings. It has been decided they are not capable of understanding how to navigate the court and make decisions. They may have intellectual or developmental disabilities, or they may have a mental illness like schizophrenia.

Bowles' official title is rehab therapist (a therapist can be connected to music, art, or recreation). She has a specific goal in working with her patients: to provide treatment to stabilize them mentally so they can go back into the court system and be successful in the courtroom. For example, if a patient can learn to focus on playing the guitar and not become frustrated and angry, it is hoped that he or she will be able to focus on what the judge is saying. Unlike other programs, she doesn't know what happens to patients when they leave. Most likely they will go back to jail until a court date can be set. She only knows what happens to them if they come back to the hospital. Often they move in and out multiple times. None of the current 370 patients in the middle group is forced to be in music—60–70 percent choose not to be in it—but the remainder come because music is their interest, and for them, it is the best course to achieve a better mental state.

Bowles' day begins with meeting members of her treatment team, which includes a psychiatrist, a psychologist, members of the nursing staff, and a social worker. She represents rehab services on a team whose scope goes beyond music therapy. In this position, she helps coordinate the service but doesn't provide the service.

In the morning, she typically meets with three to ten people in her patient group to go over their treatment plan, the goals she and her team are working on with them, the next step of action, and how she can help them to progress. She and the patients do a lot of problem solving together, using resources to provide the best plan for them.

Her therapy is using music as a tool to address goals that are nonmusical such as stress management, frustration tolerance, attention to task, and remembering information. Music is the means to help patients address those conditions, and music therapists are trained in the technical side of music to know which tools accomplish these goals.

Everyone is in the same room. Typically, in each group, there is a more prominent focus. In the guitar groups, it is playing, and it might be more structured when Bowles gives specific instruction to patients. If she notices that her plan is not working, she can change what she does, but typically they work together as a group. Bowles facilitates the experience so there aren't competing tasks within the group. She draws on the different skills of the individuals. If someone knows how to play one chord, and someone else has been playing for years, how can she address the goals of each? How can both feel successful and not compete against each other? That is the challenge if they are in the same room. When someone becomes frustrated with others' playing, Bowles comes in to bring everyone together no matter their skill level. Her skill to do this has taken some time to develop, and that was what her training was for with her internship after college (she received training for six months before she could be certified). Bowles feels she has developed this skill over the past few years by practicing it day in and day out, seeing what works and what does not.

Her biggest challenge is assessment of what the patients need, how they are doing, and what their skills and goals are. This is all done in a group setting. Bowles doesn't have the luxury of working with eight people individually and wants it be an all-inclusive experience. It takes time, and that is the difference in her training. That is something she has to focus on and know how to accomplish.

The treatments cover three broad areas: playing an instrument, listening to music, and composition or arrangement.

Playing usually involves the piano, a guitar, or a percussion instrument such as the drum or marimba. When someone wants to play something, Bowles is giving that patient a group lesson, and she must learn how to play all the instruments; that was part of the therapy training in college. She said, "I have to demonstrate proficiency with the voice, piano, guitar, and percussion. I don't progress in my education until I can demonstrate that I have the skills necessary to use those instruments in a group setting." (She can play hand drums proficiently but is not so good with the drum set, she said. That wasn't required of her, but she is learning it to assist with her work with patients.) She tries to align skills; if possible, she has people play duets. On Mondays, she works with an intermediate guitar group at 1:00 p.m. and a beginner guitar group at 2:00 p.m. She tries to make sure folks are in the appropriate group.

This is how her job differs from teaching music in schools. At the hospital, a patient's ability to play a chord doesn't matter; that is not why she is working with him. She is working with him to demonstrate that he can use that instrument and be safe with it. Even if the patient can't play the chord correctly, the goal may be to focus for five minutes.

This is different from playing in a high school orchestra when she worked on technical skills—to be able to play the right notes, at the right time with other people. She said, "That is also a component of music therapy, to provide quality musical experiences. We want the music to sound nice too." Sometimes the focus is these questions: what skills are they lacking that help them to be successful throughout life? How do they manage when they get frustrated in a guitar group? Can they manage the frustration appropriately? Do they yell? Do they walk outside and take a break? How do they manage that situation?

The nice thing, Bowles said, is that if enough patients show interest, the hospital supports buying new instruments: "We can't go out and buy thousands of dollars of instruments, but if we can justify an instrument, the hospital is very generous with the budget." She receives instruments through donations as well. If instruments aren't used, she and others move them around where they can be better utilized.

Some patients are more suited to listening to music than playing, so the therapy is geared in that direction. She and the patients work together to develop playlists of music that help the patients when they are upset or angry to cope with stress. Some music, like heavy metal, is agitating for some but may be relaxing for another. She looks for people who may want to listen together to similar types of music.

In listening, the goals are the same as with playing instruments. How does listening to music help the patients when they get frustrated? Does it reduce stress? Many times the patients know what type of music is helpful for them, as we all have music preferences. Bowles said,

> I wouldn't listen to heavy metal to help me relax, but it is very helpful to them. It is something they have experience with. I talk with the patients on how they can use these listening skills outside the hospital to help them stay safe, to keep them out of trouble with the law.

She suggests, for example, that they put headphones on and listen to music when they are frustrated instead of stealing someone's car.

Some may be more interested in composing, arranging, or working together to write lyrics and put together music for a song. Some patients who have years of experience with song writing or an instrument are extremely talented. This makes Bowles' job tricky. She deals with three to ten people who have widely different interests and skills. Some are very intelligent, but when she talks to them, their speech is disorganized, and their thoughts don't make sense. But when she gives them an instrument, they can sit down and write a song. That is an organizing experience for them.

This is what makes Bowles' job so challenging and rewarding: finding the best therapy for every individual. She loves that she is putting a piece in a puzzle. The piece may not fit, but the next one may be perfect. It is a matter of finding the right piece. If she has three patients who have different abilities, functioning levels, symptoms, and skills, how does she create an experience where they all feel successful and she can address the needs of each? Each one needs something different. That is what she loves about music therapy: she gets to be innovative, trying new things, new interventions, and finding how they can facilitate a successful experience.

Bowles feels fortunate that in the Oregon system, the administration values alternative therapies and sees the benefit for the patient.

> We have—including the Junction City hospital, which is like a sister hospital—ten music therapists: eight in Salem and two in Junction City. In addition, there are four music therapists who do not function as a therapist but are in administration or other job opportunities, so we have total of fourteen music therapists in the system.

On any day, Bowles never knows what she is going to run into. She knows the patients in her group and comes prepared, but there are times when she throws the plan out the window because of what the patients are experiencing. In that moment, what they need is different from she planned to provide. The music training she has received has been helpful, and she knows how to adapt musically to meet the needs of the patients. She said,

> Some people have no idea something is wrong with them, and they will do something off the charts. Others don't appear to have a lot of symptoms, but they may have symptoms while participating in one thing and not another. One activity may be a trigger but not another. It is a challenge but a challenge I openly accept.

She goes to work excited every day when she has the chance to help patients. How does she know they are progressing?

> I work with them pretty consistently, know them pretty well; my program is small enough with only patients who have expressed an interest in music. They don't have to be in here. By talking with people on my treatment team, finding out how others see the patients, I can from week to week see if they are progressing or not.

It is hard to quantify progress, she said, but there are two approaches to find out.

> One is quantitative research and qualitative research, putting a hard number to something versus a sense of how the patient is doing overall. With some patients, my goal is to have that patient focus in a group for five minutes. That is something I can quantify and measure. I may quantify how often the patient needs my assistance, to follow directions, how many times I am providing extra assistance. With other patients, I may do things that are more nuanced, working to improve their mood, their emotional state. Are they hunched over or sitting up straight? Are they smiling that day, and are they participating in the activity we are doing? Do they get frustrated?

She can't put a hard number on progress, but these are observable qualities that demonstrate progress.

Bowles said she has her good days and bad days. If she has a bad day, she has to intentionally take a deep breath and take two minutes to relax. When she goes into a session, she is responsible for the success of the patients and providing an environment where they can trust her, feel safe, and do something on an instrument they have never done before. If she is not in a good space with the patients, it shows.

Regardless of what kind of day Bowles has, she has someone in the room with her.

> Every day is different. Even if I have the same group of patients from week to week, a patient may have a good day, then stop taking his medication and not be able to participate the way he was before. Overall, I feel pretty safe. I have never felt in danger, although there are circumstances where safety is a concern. Everyone who works at the hospital has been trained on how to manage situations when patients might become agitated or even hostile, but I have never felt like my safety has been compromised. There are times when I am nervous about how a patient is going to respond. Is he going to throw an instrument or become aggressive?

She said that most of the patients want to be there and demonstrate safe behavior. Unlike patients who have a conviction and can be in the hospital for years, the patients in this system can only be in the hospital for a maximum of three years.

Part of Bowles' job description is to go out into the community and give talks. Not long before I met her, she made a presentation to psychology students at Western Oregon University about music therapy. She is a board member of the Oregon Association for Music Therapy (OAMT) and does extensive advocating in the community for music therapy services. Right now, she says she and her colleagues are trying to meet with people in the school districts to advocate for hiring music therapists working in special education.

At the end of our conversation, Bowles stressed how she was influenced in school, how she influenced others, and that she would not be where she is today if it were not for the many music teachers and instructors she had. She did not think she would be successful without the music component. She couldn't help patients if she did not have the right tools and the best tools possible.

She always knew music would be a part of her career but didn't know at first if she wanted to teach or to perform. The opportunity for music therapy fits both sides of her interest: the music is there, and she gets to use it to help people become better. She is that tool for them, and she could not do what she is doing now if she did not have that background.

Cynthia Richardson

When I met Cynthia Richardson, she was winding down as the North High School principal in the Salem-Keizer School District. She had been at North for seven years after serving seven additional years as the principal at nearby McKay High. Next year, she will be at the district level as director over equity, looking at programs and trying to equalize the needs of all schools. It will be a tough job, but she is passionate about giving disadvantaged students the same opportunities as those with better resources.

Music is not the lead character in Richardson's story, but it has a major supportive role. Music helped provide discipline during her teenage years and as an adult, she exhibits a special talent with her voice. She often sings solos at People's Church in northeast Salem. As the principal of North High, she gets up at school assemblies and sings songs such as *Respect, We Are Family,* and *Happy Go Lucky Girl.* She sings with the school jazz band and at the big fundraiser at the end of the year. Brian Bell, the band teacher at North, said, he could still have her come back and sing with his band.

As we shall see later, she had one more attachment to music through her son, Andre. Music has always been a fixture in her life and a way to release after a difficult day's work.

The real lead in Richardson's life was her mother, Betty Lou Haggerty, a woman with almost inhuman resolve. Richardson gained grit and determination under severe circumstances from her mom and she has had more than her share of severe circumstances.

A good example of that took place in 1997. In August of that year, Richardson moved to Salem to take a challenging position as the vice principal at McKay High School. In October she found a lump in her breast and was diagnosed with Stage 4 breast cancer. In November, she had a mastectomy. In December, her mother died, and in January, her stepmother died. During the cancer, Richardson was forced to take a leave of absence, but after six weeks, she was back at work doing supervision and all her other normal duties.

Every time Richardson came in for chemo, the doctor asked, "Have you been sick?" She said no. He said, "Well, I am going to increase your medication," and she agreed. Each time she came back for her treatment, her doctor said, "I know you have been sick," she said no, and he said, "I am going to increase your medication again." He did that three or four times and finally said, "Miss Richardson, you are a miracle. You are healed."

Richardson told me this story to help me understand that she knows she was chosen to do the work she was doing at McKay and North. Because of that, she believes the Lord is placing her in her next position as director over equity so she will be able to help kids throughout the district know they are important, give them hope, and help them believe that they can overcome obstacles and challenges and achieve their goals. Richardson doesn't believe "the Lord gives you any more than you can bear." She has asked for wisdom, and with her past jobs, she will get that wisdom. It will be made clear, and she will have the resources to do what she has been appointed to do in this season of her life.

Her entire time in Salem has been in schools attended by students in poverty. Over a four-year period at North High, only 68.1 percent of the students graduated; counteracting that rate has been a huge challenge. North has 67 percent minority students, 48 percent are in the English Language Learning (ELL) program, 77 percent are eligible for free and reduced lunch, and 14 percent have disabilities. Many students can't graduate in four years, because they are credit deficient when they come in. Often they aren't able to take certain classes until they have a good understanding of the English language. These students go home and don't have anyone who can help them—their parents didn't necessarily graduate from high school. Some students are from a migrant population and need to travel with their parents. Richardson said the migrant population has been reduced, but some families still work the fields and move to work other fields. Some families are dysfunctional, and the school deals with medical complications such as diabetes.

Richardson and her staff strike at the problems in different ways. For kids who cannot graduate in four years, she has a five-year plan. North provides summer school to help deficient students graduate in a timely fashion. Teachers are given training to help individual students, and students are encouraged to receive the additional instruction. Because many of them don't have technology at home, the library has extended hours during the week or on Saturdays to give them the opportunity to use the resources. In classes with more than thirty-five students, some who are struggling can go to another room for one-on-one homework assistance. North has a Parent University that gives parents the training and resources to help their children.

Students can take certain classes that provide college credit, which reduces the amount of money they will need when they go to college. They may say they can't take the classes because they have to work to make money and don't have time to do the extra reading. To help these students, Richardson and her staff implemented an advanced placement support class that is not a study hall. An AP teacher instructs, and the kids receive help and have the time to do the necessary reading. Richardson tries to get the best people to teach and help the kids navigate the system and work toward college. She said,

> Individuals still need the determination, perseverance, and grit. I came from poverty. I have been poor, but I don't have to act like it. I don't have to remain in that status. If I work hard, if I set goals and achieve them, I can rise to another level. We have to be able to give kids hope, sit down with them, and help them set goals. They have to see that those goals are attainable.

One of the most important ways kids can succeed is to be in extracurricular activities. Richardson said,

> Students in extracurricular activities have a much higher graduation rate. Our data shows that students who are involved in extracurricular activities—sports, music, drama, or any other activity—tend to do better. One of the reasons they do better with athletics is because if they don't pass the classes and meet qualifications, they can't be in sports. That is a motivating factor.

Many students who would like to be in these activities cannot. They come from families of poverty and must go home and babysit so their parents can go work. Some kids have to work to help pay the expenses at home. Richardson said,

> They can't be involved in extracurricular activities like they want to. Hopefully they don't miss school for work. Sometimes the inability to get into extracurricular activities is huge. These kids may want to take part but can't.

Just to be in music is special for many of the kids at North.

> Our choir, band, orchestra kids are normally our higher-end kids. Most of them have started programs early in elementary and middle school, and it has carried over with them. They are the elite of the school. I have seen changes in students. I can tell you that in band, kids are here at all times of the night, doing extra rehearsals, all kinds of practices. Choir is the same. We are constantly trying to find ways to support our band, choir, and orchestra so the kids can get to all the contests. Whoever sits in this chair has to be very creative with funding, has to have great relationships with community. We are fortunate to have the North High Alumni Association. Steve Chambers, who is president, is remarkable in how he raises money.

CYNTHIA RICHARDSON WAS MIRED IN GRINDING POVERTY AS AN African American growing up in Tyler, Texas, a medium-sized city between Dallas and Shreveport, Louisiana. She was born in 1956 in the culture that permeated the South before the Civil Rights Movement. Her parents were teachers, but in those days, schools were still segregated. Her parents had to go outside of Tyler to get jobs; her mother traveled sixty-six miles northeast to teach in Daingerfield, and her father drove 121 miles northwest to his job in McKinney. When Richardson was four years old, her parents divorced, and her mother became the sole provider. Although she owned a house in Tyler, because Betty Lou had to teach so far away in Daingerfield, she rented a house there for the family to stay in during the week. They came back to Tyler on weekends and in the summer. Betty Lou was forced to make payments for the rental in Daingerfield and the home in Tyler, with no help from Dad for the finances. Cynthia said,

> Mom taught and raised three girls by herself. There was no money left over, but we didn't know it. We didn't know we were poor, because my mother sacrificed. She sewed and made beautiful uniforms. I was a majorette in high school; my sister was a cheerleader. These were additional expenses, but she made our uniforms. She made our prom dresses. We always had enough food. My mother cooked all the time. She cooked three well-nourished, well-prepared meals every day. We normally ate a school lunch, and my mother paid for the school lunch. It was not that expensive at that time, but she paid for it. When we weren't in school, she made sure we had a hot meal for lunch. I look back at everything my mother did, and I am still amazed. She worked all the time and did what she needed to do for us to have what we needed to have.

Richardson started taking band in sixth grade, playing the flute until she graduated from high school. (She doesn't remember where the instrument came from; probably someone gave it to her.) She was a majorette in sixth through eighth grade, and by ninth grade, along with being a majorette, she was a twirler. She needed to have a band uniform and extra uniforms to be a majorette. She performed at all of the football games, and her mother made all of the uniforms. She said,

> I have two sisters, and we talk all the time about what our mother did. We came to believe there was no reason why people should not be able to make it. It becomes the decisions we make, what we choose to do with our resources, and how we manage them.

The schools in Daingerfield were segregated when Betty Lou taught home economics at Rhodes High School, but the administrators developed a step-by-step integration process that apparently worked well. They began by switching teachers: some white teachers were willing to teach in black schools and vice versa. Richardson remembered having her first white teacher in the fourth grade, and by the time she was in sixth grade, the schools were totally integrated. Rhodes High School was made a junior high, and Richardson went to Daingerfield High.

This integration was not universal, especially outside of school. During Richardson's time in Daingerfield, when she went to a movie, she was forced to sit in the back with the other African Americans. When she was in high school, she was the only African American twirler majorette. She said,

> On Fridays when we had pep assemblies, we would always go downtown to the 5 & 10 cent store to buy the little bags and everything, but when we went into a store, the clerks would always watch me because I was black. The other girls were not watched. They did whatever they wanted to do.

Even when Richardson was a majorette, she continued to play the flute. That was a requirement to be a majorette; you had to be part of the band. Being in music gave her more structure. There were rehearsals in the evenings; she had to make a commitment to be at the band hall and the football field to rehearse, and that kept her from being idle and getting into trouble.

Richardson was also in the National Honor Society and vice president of the student body her junior and senior years. During her senior year, she led a sit-out.

We wanted an African American band to play at our prom and were told no. We were integrated, but we gave up our school name (Rhodes), our school colors; we had to inherit everything that Daingerfield High School already had. We came together, but being in the same building, having the same resources doesn't necessarily give you the same opportunities. For example, I was never in an honors class. They wouldn't let me, so there were lots of problems, and there still are. There still are in Salem.

I led a sit-out where my mother taught. We wanted this band, but every time we had anything, it was always what the whites wanted. We made up our minds we wanted something for the upcoming prom that resembled us one last time. After the sit-out, they let us have our band. It was strictly an African American band, the kind of music we could relate to. The group was called the Soulphadelics, full of soul music. The white kids ended up liking the soul music. After I graduated, I didn't follow up on it, but I think they listened to the black kids more and allowed them to embed things that were important to them into the school.

Richardson never picked up her flute again after she graduated from high school, but she continued to sing in her church choir in Tyler. By the time she was thirty-two and pregnant with her youngest son, a lady came in from west Texas to be the new choir director at her church.

She walked up to me and said,

"I want you to do this solo."

"I don't sing solos."

"But I want you to sing this solo."

"Okay."

I did the solo, and the lady said, "You are very gifted and talented."

No one before ever told me I could sing. I sang in the church choir, but when I moved to Lancaster, Texas near Dallas, I was in church but not involved in music. Then I got a new job in Lincoln, Nebraska—by this time, my baby was seven years old. One day he came home with a flyer and said,

"Mom, I want to try out for this." It was the part of Travis in

Raisin in the Sun.

I said, "Okay." I always promoted my kids or supported them in whatever they wanted to do. I was the high school assistant principal. and I made sure I was off that night. I didn't have any supervision duties and took him to the tryout. During the tryout, the director looked at me and said,

"Ma'am, will you come read with him so he can feel comfortable?"

So I got up and read. Later the director said, "Everyone who is going to be in the next round, I will call tomorrow."

I got a call the next day at work, and he said,

"Miss Richardson, I want you to come back for tryouts tonight."

"I didn't try out. I was reading with my son."

He said, "Oh, you and your son come back tonight."

So I went back that night. My son didn't get a part, but the director offered me the leading role as Mama. I had never acted in my life. That is the hardest work in the whole wide world, to try to work full time, have two kids, and learn a leading role for a play. My son went to every rehearsal and sat on the front row for every show.

Both my parents had gone to a historical black college in Tyler called Texas College. It is still there today and is still predominantly black. A high school home economics teacher who worked with my mother told her, "Do not allow Cynthia to go to an all-black school. She needs to go to an integrated college where she will have better opportunities. She will be limited if she goes to an African American school." My mom would not let me go to Texas College, so I applied to East Texas State in Commerce, got admitted, loaded my little car—I had a car by this time, which my grandfather bought me; it was a 1967 Mustang (this was in 1975)—and went to East Texas State. I unloaded everything in my room and was shocked when I got there. Everyone said, "We are going to have a party tonight. Come to such and such a place." I went to that place, and there were so much drugs and alcohol, it scared me to death. I went back to my room, loaded up my car the next day, and came back home. My mom wouldn't let me in the house. She said, "You are going to school." I said, "I want to go to school but not there."

I had a girlfriend who had a house with some friends; I stayed with her and enrolled at Tyler Junior College. I was back home but not with my mom. I don't even know how I paid for it. I worked at Sears all that summer, and I must have gotten some kind of financial aid. I don't remember. I took eighteen to twenty-one hours a term, because I could pay for it as I went, and I was trying to acquire as many credits as I could. I always knew I was going to be a teacher. I wanted to be a home economics teacher like my mom. I graduated from TJC in one and a half years but needed to continue on in college to get my degree in teaching.

This time, I went to North Texas State in Denton, enrolling there in January of 1977. My mother and grandmother took me to the dorm to get set up, and as we were walking in, we discovered it was a co-ed dorm. I didn't know anyone, so I didn't sign up for a roommate. My roommate was a very affluent white girl. She was as shocked as I was. She was very privileged and probably had a maid to take care of her, because she was nasty, mess all over the floor. I thought, *I cannot live with her*, but she stayed with her boyfriend a lot and was never there. At the end of that term, she moved out of the dorm. By this time, I decided I wanted to pledge a sorority, so I went into an African American sorority house called the Alpha Kappa Alfas. I moved over to the sorority house, still working at Sears in Denton and still taking as many credits as I could possibly take. I don't remember that the sorority was more expensive than the dorm, but I got financial aid. I had graduated from high school in 1975 and college in 1978, three years with $10,000 in loans.

I decided I needed to teach. I had a boyfriend at Angelo State University in San Angelo out in the desert of west Texas. He wanted me to move there. I knew a girl who lived there and I moved in with her. I immediately enrolled in grad school to work on my master's. I also worked at a bank as a teller; I always had a job because I didn't want that burden on my mom. I moved there in August of 1978 and completed the term in May of 1979.

In August of that year, I got a call to teach at Robert E. Lee High School in Tyler. When I went and interviewed, the principal looked at me and said, "I have a home ec program that is dying. We just built this beautiful building, there are four teachers down there, and they are killing the program. We need someone who will go and turn this program around." In Tyler, there were two high schools: Robert E. Lee, predominantly white and John Tyler, mostly black. I was hired to go into the white culture at Robert E. Lee. I was shocked to have the job, but I went there and became the rookie teacher of the year. I taught at Robert E. Lee for eleven years with standing room only in my classes.

By now I was ready to be an administrator. I had finished my administration credentials at the University of Texas at Tyler. I started my master's at San Angelo but finished at University of Texas at Tyler, so I have two master's degrees: one in health and PE and one in education with an emphasis on administration. By that time I was married, going to school, while working full time with two kids.

I interviewed in Lancaster, Texas. The superintendent wanted me—he really didn't have a job for me, but he created a position called administrative assistant over student services. I was a truant officer for the district. I did a lot of going out to homes and stressing the importance of why kids who had bad attendance needed to be in school.

I did that for a year and at the end of that year, when the elementary principal retired, because I had been so effective in getting kids to school and handling discipline with kids, the school people asked me to become their principal. Basically Lancaster was at the beginning of integrating the district. There had been white flight; now African Americans were coming into Lancaster. Teachers were not accustomed to working with African Americans, so I had the opportunity of mediating for African American families, whose voices weren't heard enough in the school and who didn't know how to navigate the system. I had never seen an elementary school in my journey, but I was there two years, and the first year, I received an award from the governor, because we turned around the academics in the school.

I transferred to the high school in Lancaster, a predominantly white school. The district hired a new high school principal, and I was hired to be his assistant principal. I went there and did what they asked me to do. Within my second year, I was on bus duty one day—I will never forget that day—the day care had just dropped off my two kids. They always came to the high school, because I always had games right after school. I had just opened this glass door to let them into my office when all of a sudden glass went everywhere. I turned around to look and a high school girl had shot another high school girl right there on the school grounds. The principal always had a habit of going home early, so I had someone call him to have him come back, and I called 911.

After that, I was recruiting for Lancaster and in that role went to a big education fair in Louisiana. This woman from Lincoln, Nebraska, kept looking at me and said,

"I really like you, can I take you to dinner tonight?"

"Sure."

"We went to dinner, and the woman said, "You know, we could really use someone like you in Lincoln."

"I don't know anything about Nebraska."

"We could really use someone like you in administration."

"I don't think so."

I went back to work, and the woman called and said, "The superintendent wants to meet you. Is there any way you could come out so we could introduce you to him?"

I said, "If I come, it has to be the whole family, because I want them to be a part of this."

My husband was with the post office, so he could move like that. We had moved to Lancaster for him, because he wanted an opportunity to advance. When we went to Lincoln, they offered me a significant raise and were willing to pay for my moving expenses. We said yes.

In 1995, I became the assistant principal at Lincoln High School. I truly loved it there. That is where I learned about diversity. In Texas, I only knew about blacks and whites. In the part of Texas where I was, there weren't even many Hispanics. When I went to Lincoln, we had the Muslims, we had all kinds. Many of them were refugees. The Catholic Social Services was taking them in. We had to have a room for prayer, a sink for them to wash their hands, certain menus available for them, so that is where I started learning about different cultures. I hadn't been exposed to it.

By the end of the school year in 1997, I had been asked to go to Detroit for a recruiting fair, and the Salem-Keizer table was right across from my table. They invited me to go to dinner with them. I was happy in Lincoln except for the snow and freezing to death, so Salem-Keizer talked me into flying out for an interview in New Mexico to meet the superintendent, Kay Baker. Meeting the superintendent at a conference in New Mexico was not odd if you understood the politics in Salem at the time. I was the first former high school principal they would interview, so it was not odd. It all depends on whose perspective you are looking at. (She laughed.) They brought me in to interview for the McNary High School principal position. There were thirty-some people in the interview room. I was the surprise candidate. They already knew who they wanted for the position: Ed John, who was known in the district. At the time, they were having problems with a principal they hired at Sprague, a guy from California who they had to dismiss. I don't think they were willing to take a risk, bringing someone in from the outside at that time, so they met with me and asked me to please consider coming in as an assistant principal. I asked, "Why would I come here to be an assistant principal? I'm not interested in moving across the country for that." One lady spoke to me and said, "You need to come to Salem and learn the culture before you try to lead it." Those were words of wisdom that I could never pay enough money to have. There are very few African Americans in Salem. This is a big difference when you come from a place like Tyler, Texas, or Dallas and you have seen black mayors and superintendents. My expectation is that African Americans can be wherever they want to be and do whatever they want to do.

They talked me into coming to McKay to be the assistant principal when I had originally applied for the McNary position. I was at McKay for one and a half years when I said to the district, "I can't work for this principal," so they placed me as principal at Adam Stephens Middle School. McKay reopened in a couple of years for a high school principal position. I was asked to apply but never did. The day the application period was going to close, the superintendent came in, met with me and said, "You really need to apply for that." She talked to me a long time. She said, "I would really be disappointed if at the end of the day you had not submitted your application for this position," so right before the deadline, I walked in with my application.

At that time, North was open, McKay was open, and McNary was open. Ed John went to West. All three positions had interviews. After my interview with McKay, I received unanimously all thirty votes. They wanted me back. At North, the interview committee had to do a second round, McNary a second round, and eventually John Honey was named for North and Ken Parschal for McNary. All of us served seven years, and at the end of the seven years, we all got moved. I was moved to North, John moved to McNary, and Ken moved to McKay.

Now after seven more years, I am moving again. I truly love being in Salem. I have no desire to go back to Texas. Both of my boys graduated from McKay while I was there. The youngest, Andre, was very, very talented in music. He was in a lot of plays in high school and always part of the Honors Choir, Best of the Northwest, all of that, then he went to study music at Wayne State University in Detroit. During his freshman year at McKay, Paul Myers was the choir director. Andre sang a solo for him, and Paul said, "That is all wrong, all wrong. That is not the way you sing it." Andre had sung from his culture in Texas. Andre came home and said,

"Mom, I'm quitting choir."

"Why?"

"The choir director doesn't think I have talent."

"Tell me what happened."

He told me, and I said, "You don't quit, honey, you don't quit."

Andre said, "Well, he wants me to sing a different way."

I said, "That is learning the correct way. You need to be obedient and do it. You can do your style of music in church." We belonged to a black church at that time, and they let him sing all the time. He was on praise and worship teams.

I asked, "How are you going to major in music in college when you don't have any experience in high school? How are you going to compete with kids who have taken music classes in high school and then go to college?"

He didn't hear me.

The next year, I became the principal at McKay. Paul Myers left, and before the fall of 1997, Karl Raschkes hired Eugene Rogers. Eugene came in, an African American man, got into Andre's face, and said, "This is what you have to do to make it in the music industry. You need to learn the core music and learn how to sing it correctly, learn how to read music." He really spoke to Andre. Eugene and his wife became Andre's godparents. Eugene would have stayed here, but his wife was miserable. She was from Detroit, and he left to please her, but Andre went with him. He was going to be a junior.

How did I feel? I prayed about it and I was going with that is not what I wanted to do, but I ended up going to Cancun that summer. My older son, Prince, graduated from high school, and it was his graduation trip. I met this lady, and while we were sitting there talking, she looked at me and said, "You know, we as black mamas really hinder our boys." I looked at her because she completely changed the subject. She said, "You need to learn how to cut the string and allow them to have experiences." I wondered, God, did you send her here to talk to me? After that, I let him go.

Andre went to Detroit his junior year and stayed with the Rogers family. By Thanksgiving, Andre called me and said, "Mom, I really want to come back home. I miss being at home. I loved it that I got into one of the music academies, but Eugene doesn't have kids, and I am miserable. They don't know how to raise kids. I love my school, I love the people, but I want to come home.

I said, "You can come home."

"I don't want to feel like a failure."

"It is not a failure to go experiment with something and decide that you want to come back and finish up the traditional way."

He came back.

By this time, the choir teacher was Gretchen Longwell. She was at McKay until Stanford Scriven took over. She decided to move on; she got tired of the struggle. She was very knowledgeable.

Andre was a music major for three years at Wayne State. He started getting really involved, had a manager, did some things with Usher and different other people in the music industry, but he found out that you have to have money to make money. He was innocent, had lived with me most of his life, and he got out into that and found out he didn't want that kind of hustle-bustle life. I wish I could have been there with him to help oversee his career. I have some beautiful newspaper articles, but he quit and now works for Delta Airlines. He is a flight attendant; he was in Greece last week and he is on his way to London today. He goes wherever he wants to go and has a beautiful voice, but he chose not to pursue music. I don't know what happened in his life, but when you are given a gift and talent, you have to use it the way God gave it to you to use it. When he left gospel and went into R&B, it was the route God wanted him to take. He now says he has been doing recordings; I haven't heard them. I believe he will turn back to music and love it.

Prince is not involved in music. He got his degree at Linfield College in elementary education and married a girl who is a manager for Mary Kay Cosmetics. She is a manager for a Mac Cosmetics store in Belleview, Washington. They have two children. The year he graduated was the year we had the big layoffs in education, so he worked several different jobs. Right now, he is in the corporate office for Tire Buyer in sales, but he will find his way back to the classroom, because he is very good with kids.

My mother had a beautiful voice, but she was very shy and didn't use it in public. My father sang in a quartet and has an album. My grandfather, my dad's dad, was really big in church music—he sung in choirs in churches. Years ago, I use to drive him to church meetings. When I ended up at the junior college, I moved in with my grandmother, my dad's mom. She had a 2:00 a.m. curfew. I would get off at 9:00 p.m. and be home at 10:00 p.m. to do homework. She cooked for me, did my laundry; she was a retired English teacher. She approved all of my papers. I always lived with education and knew how important it was.

I love it right now. This is a huge part of my life. Music gives me a lot of peace away from my job. I always had education and always had music. What has singing done for me? At People's

Church, they do a huge production every Christmas; I have been one of the soloists selected for the past two years. At People's, if you ask about Cynthia Richardson, they think I am—what did one lady say? "A songbird."

Pamela Miller

Pam Miller passed away on July 2, 2016. She is the only person (thus far) on my list who is no longer with us. If you knew her, as I did, you would understand there was no one remotely like her. Some time ago, her name was submitted for a Best Music Teacher of the Year award, but the submission was rejected because she did not teach in a public school. What a shame! The school music programs in Salem would be in a dreary mess without her and her fellow piano teachers.

Miller taught not only piano but organ and, at one point, the harpsichord. Her sister, Carolyn, said in the funeral eulogy that Miller was a teaching machine. Was she ever! She taught up to eighty lessons a week, all seven days. She had sixty to sixty-five students each year, but some of these students took both piano and organ.

Miller's work day normally began in the early afternoon but sometimes late morning, because many of her students were homeschooled. She then took other students after school and often worked as late as 10:00 p.m.—it wasn't until after that she would microwave a frozen meal. On Sundays, she taught her students from the Seventh Day Adventist church.

This work was not drudgery for Miller. She thrived on it. People in the next room listening to her teach often heard her laughing with her students, but she was a disciplinarian. She was picky about which students she took and demanded that they be diligent. She told me that she loved Asian students because they *practiced*. With other students, she was exasperated, even angry on rare occasions, if they hadn't put in the time at home. She could be stymied if one student in a family worked hard but a sibling did not. In these circumstances, she might put up with the apathy or tactfully suggest that "Justin" had a better future in soccer. She was in these situations because parents had all their children taking lessons from her, and she might go through five or six siblings before the youngest graduated.

Miller took a month off every August and grew restless as the days went by. She could not wait to get back to teaching, but she did not idle her time away. Before online transactions took over, she went to Sheet Music Service in Portland and spent hours there, days even, and paid hundreds of dollars for the music her students would learn throughout the entire year. She was saddened when Sheet Music Service closed down. Once the music was purchased, she spent untold additional hours preparing a special notebook for each student, placing the requisite sheet music inside along with a calendar of events.

In addition to teaching, Miller was the organist on Sunday mornings at First Presbyterian Church. She accompanied the church choir and played for countless weddings and funerals. She hated funerals with open microphone because she never knew how long they would last. "Uncle George" would stand up, telling his life story, while students outside her home were waiting for lessons, but she was paid to be at the funeral. She couldn't leave, because there would be a closing hymn and postlude music. Fortunately, her students and parents were flexible and willing to reschedule the lesson. She never had problems with parents because they regarded her so highly.

Miller never married. It is hard to imagine any man fitting into her schedule. She had no social life to speak of away from music. All of it was channeled into the organizations she belonged to: the Federated Music Club, Oregon Music Teachers' Association (OMTA), and the American Guild of Organists. She came to the meetings for all three organizations and was often a state officer.

Connie Snyder, a good friend and fellow piano teacher, said Pam was the bulwark of piano teachers' organizations before Snyder moved to Salem in the late 1980s. Snyder said,

> Everyone knew if Pam didn't decide to enter something for a festival, you might as well forget having that event, but she always entered students. That is the way it was, and some people were jealous because her students won everything, and they deserved to.
>
> Pam was the person who researched everything for the National Federated Club, who figured out how a kid could get a gold cup, bigger and bigger trophies until one student got the hugest gold cup you could imagine. She made that all happen. Other teachers didn't know about it. You could get larger trophies, and the way you could do it was by doing a solo and a concerto. It is a really neat system, and it really meant a lot to the kids who participated.
>
> If some of the more active teachers had thirty to forty student entries in a festival, Miller would have ninety to a hundred. At Federated festivals, many of her students played both solos and concertos. These concertos were duets: the student would play the solo and Pam would play the orchestra reduction (a piano arrangement) of the orchestra. Other teachers might have two or three concertos in a festival; Miller would regularly have thirty. She would play every orchestra reduction in every duet. Some of these reductions were simple for younger children, but many were difficult and taxing to learn. The entire orchestration was written alongside, but Miller played them flawlessly. She was an unbelievable sight-reader.

Karen Kohne, another good friend of Miller's who subbed playing the organ at the Presbyterian Church when Pam was gone, said,

> My daughter, Heidi, took organ from Pam. She did some of the Gene Williams concertos. They were charming, very easy, but the kids felt like they were playing Rachmaninoff. Some were Mozart, still easy, but some, when they were competing for competitions, were playing Tchaikovsky and Chopin. In some of the later years

> for competitions, she would hire another woman to do some of the accompaniments. It got to the point that some of the kids were so good she finally said, ah, she would get someone else to accompany. She was so nervous for the really hard ones for a competition.

Miller involved her students in the Wiscarson Competition, the Federated Festival, the OMTA Bach Festival and the OMTA syllabus, which required a student to be in a room performing in front of an adjudicator. Most of these events took place in the Bach Room at the back of Weather's Music in south Salem. Kohne said,

> The festivals in the Bach Room went on for two weeks, three weeks. Pam spent so much of her life in the Bach Room, it was her home away from home. If she counted the hours she was there, she would have spent years in the Bach Room. When Weathers announced the store would close, Willy (Karen's husband) thought it would be nice to purchase the Bach Room sign over the entrance door and give it to Pam. When he approached Keith Weathers with the idea, Keith insisted Willy would have the sign for no cost. Keith regarded Pam well; he was very fond of her. Willy took the sign down from above the door and we gave it to her for a birthday present. She posted the sign in her studio.

When Weather's Music closed, Miller bought the sheet music bins and installed them in a room next to her studio. She now had a new home for her vast collection of sheet music.

If the festivals were held at Weather's Music, her recitals were always at First Presbyterian Church. She had so many students perform that her spring recitals were held on two evenings. At these end-of-the-year recitals, there was always a table in front holding beautiful programs and all the gold cups. Miller made presentations, and everyone got certificates and cups.

As important and well-organized as the end-of-the-year recitals became, Miller's Christmas recitals were legendary. Kohne said,

> The Christmas recitals were events to witness. We would go even after our kids weren't taking just because we knew they were going to be wonderful. She did not split up the Christmas

recital; it lasted forever. The kids got dressed up; they were in their Christmas finery. Girls were in velvet dresses; boys all had shirts and ties. They got the message: this was going to be a fancy event, something the students should take pride in. Pam taught stage presence; she didn't just teach the music. She said, "Even if they don't clap for you, you show confidence when you go on stage. You sit at the piano and wait before you put your hands on the keys. You are to bow, you do the whole presentation." There was always a theme for the Christmas recital: perhaps stars, angels, or the three kings. Whatever the theme, she would pick all the pieces for everyone based on the theme. The programs would have the themes with stars and so forth. She had beautifully printed programs.

One thing that made the recitals so long was that Pam knew about other instruments the kids played. If someone was a flutist or played the violin, they played the instrument, and she had other students accompany them. She taught accompanying also. We would have instrumental solos and maybe the two kids would trade off, one playing the instrument and one accompanying on the piano. She had choral numbers: the kids would be organized into little choirs. Maybe all boys would have an octet. She had all these extra rehearsals, rehearsals for the little boys' octet and so forth, and of course she never charged for the recital. When you had vocal, instrumental, piano, and organ recitations, it would be a three-hour concert and then refreshments afterwards. That was my present to her for her birthday. I would put on the reception after the recital, doing the table decorations and food, although parents wanted to bring food. The Christmas recitals were spectacular.

THIS HUMAN DYNAMO WAS BORN IN KENTUCKY TO PARENTS WHO were not musicians but successful business people. When Pam was five and Carolyn eight, their mother announced to them that she was going to buy a piano. She asked, "Will you practice if I buy a piano?" Without giving it any thought, they said yes. The family lived in an apartment over the business and there was no way to bring the piano up the narrow staircase. It had to be brought through the window into the living room. That was Pam's first experience with the piano. She and Carolyn were signed up with Mr. Buchanan, and from then on, neither had to be reminded to practice. "We just took to it," Carolyn said.

In high school, the sisters were fortunate to have a wonderful music professor who was an organist but also taught the music classes. Pam wanted to take organ lessons. The professor encouraged the sisters to go to a university with a strong music program: Carolyn chose Oberlin in Ohio and Pam followed. They both got master's degrees in California, close to their grandparents. There they diverged: Carolyn went to University of Southern California, but Pam attended Redlands University because of its strong organ department. Pam always considered the organ her first instrument.

After Miller graduated, she knew she would teach; that was all she wanted to do. She stayed in Los Angeles, going to areas like Bel Air or Hollywood Hills teaching children of the rich and famous. She entered their homes and often never saw the parents—the governess answered the door.

In 1984, Miller visited Salem with a boyfriend; she fell in love with the city and never looked back. When she arrived in Salem, she landed the organist position at Church of Christ Scientist south of downtown. She played there for three years and loved it. Kohne said,

> They appreciated Pam's music, were very complimentary, paid well, but she left because they wouldn't let her teach organ at the church. No one could touch that organ except the organist. She was already building a piano clientele in her studio, but she also wanted to teach organ, wanted to teach in the sanctuary, and they said no. They didn't want anyone else there. They didn't want the traffic—other people would dirty up the organ.

Meanwhile in Salem, a group of women musicians formed a study group called The Sounding Board. They met once a month at someone's home. A small lunch was provided followed by a forty-five minute program featuring one member who would perform to prepare for a recital or a new piece for an audience. The others made helpful comments. Kohne was one of the members when Miller started attending. She hadn't been in Salem long and they hardly knew each other at the time.

Kohne was a freelance organist; she had played at Christian Science Church and other venues including First Presbyterian. She was primarily a cellist but asked the current organist at First Presbyterian, Ruth Million, if she would give her lessons. Million became ill with a ruptured appendix, and Kohne was pushed into the position until the church could hire someone to take Million's place. After several months, Miller came to apply. Kohne said jokingly, "You can have the organist position but only if you will teach my son." Miller agreed and was the First Presbyterian organist for twenty-nine years. Kohne subbed for her, and the two became fast friends—"like sisters," Karen said. They talked on the phone frequently, and Willie always knew when Pam was on the line because Karen would be laughing. Normally others would not get her to do that during a phone conversation.

Miller was the leading member of the Federated Music Club when Snyder moved to Salem. Snyder said,

> Pam was very helpful. She helped me learn the ropes, how to do the music festival, how to enter the concerto division and do concertos with students. She would let me visit her music library and sometimes we played concertos together. She talked me into a lot of things for which I am not sorry. If she wasn't such a great person, she would have intimidated the lights out of me, but she was nothing but encouraging and building. "You can do this," she would say. I realized we were musically on the same page, that we wanted really quality things. We became really good friends.

Snyder and Miller had other things in common:

> We got along well, because we are both politically conservative. She was a night owl and loved certain TV shows such *as The Good Wife* and *24* with Kiefer Sutherland. When we worked together,

> I would say, "Pam, you are just going to have to trust me on this," because that is what Sutherland always said on the show.

Snyder's daughter, Kristen, was legally blind, but she wanted to take organ lessons from Miller. Kristen said to Pam, "I have always wanted to play the organ. Could you teach me?" Kristen had a good ear. Snyder said,

> What Pam did for her is the most unbelievable teaching anyone could ever do. She said, "I would be happy to. We will go to First Presbyterian," and right off the bat, she said, "Okay, Kristen, we are going to enter you in the festival." Kristen earned a gold cup, because Pam entered her in the adult organ division every year. Kristen could never see the music, but she could instantly memorize. Pam would say, "Okay, we are going to do this. You do this and start here, and we are going to play this section." Bit by bit, hand by hand, then add the foot pedals—that is how she taught Kristen.
>
> When we would leave the First Presbyterian Church, Pam was always uplifting. It is difficult to describe music to another person and have them learn to play it. There are lots of senses you can't use, and it is hard. Pam didn't give Kristen easy stuff. The strongest word Pam ever used when she was frustrated in trying to help Kristen was "mercy." Kristen would say, "Hey, Mom, I worked really hard, and Pam didn't have to say mercy once." She didn't say the word loud either. She would say it and laugh. We would all laugh.

Miller was able to purchase a beautiful, three-level home. She was the only person living there, but no room was wasted. One bedroom was decorated for her niece when she came up from Eugene to stay. Another was specifically for Carolyn when she flew up from Florida. Miller gave me a tour several years ago, and all rooms were used for one project or another. In and around the studio in the basement, there were plenty of music associations. The wallpaper in a nearby bathroom was filled with sheet music scores; the code to the house was Bach's birth year. Students walked through her three-car garage, stepped briefly back outside and in again through a back door leading to a waiting room with an upright piano for warm up. The waiting room had wallpaper with music motif and photographs showing Miller with past students. Miller had two grand pianos side by side in a lovely teaching studio overlooking the back garden. A third grand piano that she inherited stood unused in a nearby room, and she also owned a harpsichord (at one time, she had two). Some years ago, she had the harpsichord shipped away to have a traditional baroque-era mural painted on the underside of the lid. She owned an organ with a full set of pedals, but she taught all organ lessons at First Presbyterian Church ("First Prez," as most people call it).

Miller had a beautiful kitchen with two ovens, but she never cooked. Friends jokingly suggested that she use the ovens to store music, because they would never be used for baking. She didn't even like making coffee at home; instead traveled to McDonalds for a cup. Miller told Snyder there were two things she vowed never to do: make a pie crust and change a diaper. Without a doubt, she kept both promises.

Before her present house, Miller was down the street in a home almost as grand. I had been in the studio there and concluded, as others did, that the house was all anyone would ever need. Nevertheless, Miller wanted to live in another house, something more suitable. Kohne said,

> We got to know her really well when it came time for her to find a new house. Willy said, "Pam, why do you need another house?" Her other house had the same kind of arrangement, not nearly as big, but it had a ground floor that had a wonderful teaching studio with an outside entrance. It was great, but now she wanted one more house in her life. She got one realtor who, driving her around, showed her houses that weren't any bigger or nicer than the one she had, so Pam fired her. All this time, Willy kept saying, "Pam, why do you need a bigger house?" One day, she called and said, "I found a great house. Would you come and look at it? I need both of your opinions." Willy wasn't available right then,

> but I went to look at it, planning on repeating what Willy had always said. We drove over but not with a realtor. I don't know how we got in, but I opened the front door and said, "Pam, this is your house." There was something about it. I hadn't even been downstairs—in fact had only the briefest look. We went through the entire house, and I loved it. I came home and told Willy. "Oh." Willy said, "You women!" I said, "You go." He went with Pam, and it was the same thing. He opened the door and knew this was her house. I never thought I would hear Willy say it. He said, "This is your house." There was something about the house that day; both of us knew it from the time we walked in the door. I don't know what it was.

There were several things that Miller would not do or did not like to do. As mentioned, she almost never cooked except to put a meal in the microwave. She had someone come in and clean her house. She had no appetite for traveling; she flew to see her sister in Florida over Christmas vacation, but she dreaded the flight. Beyond the mechanics of traveling, she had little interest in tourism. It would seem, except for having nice things in her home, that she had no life aside from music.

Except for gardening.

Miller loved to garden. She would get her old station wagon to haul plants, travel to Egan's in Keizer to buy hundreds of annuals and plant them around the edge of her back yard. She loved plants arranged in pots, mostly sitting on her back deck outside the studio, but her home was next to a creek where deer lived. They ate her flowers, which discouraged her.

She wore blue jeans while she worked outside, but no one except for a woman she hired to help her with her gardening ever saw her wearing jeans. Even her closest friends never saw her in her garden gear.

On one occasion when she was carrying a flat of plants, she slipped on the wet grass and broke her ankle. She couldn't walk downstairs to teach in her studio, but you couldn't keep this woman down. She rented a piano from Weather's Music and taught lessons on the main floor in her laundry room for several months until her ankle healed sufficiently and she could walk downstairs.

Miller never stopped working, but in 2014, she was diagnosed with cancer. She told no one except Carolyn and made her swear to secrecy. She took treatments for the cancer and thought it was cured, but she went back for a checkup and the doctors found more cancer. She was devastated. Finally she was so sick that she had to cancel lessons for a time, but she had her end-of-the-year recital on June 12, 2016, and was determined to go through with it. She had all these students she was so close to and she wanted to see them one last time. Carolyn flew up from Florida to help her. On the night of the recital, she rebounded. She was her cheery self; no one could tell anything was wrong with her. At the end, she stood up before everyone and told them she could not have done the recital without them. The evening ended, and three weeks later, she was gone.

All these students had taken lessons from Miller, and suddenly they were cut adrift. One parent I talked to had a real struggle finding another teacher for her child. It took her months to find someone who even approached Miller's qualities.

Pam Miller was one of a kind. She was brilliant, she was a workhorse, she loved finery, and yet she was warm and funny. One story told at the funeral may encapsulate her as much as any. She had a next-door neighbor, Julius Liang, a teenager who had taken lessons from her for several years. Unlike Miller, Julius hated gardening, but he agreed to help her one day because she had done so many things for him. For three hours he was out there getting dirty; he said he was head to toe in dirt. It was time for him to come into Pam's home for lunch—she had sent him to Burger King for food. She even gave him a bottle of Coca-Cola and promised not to tell his mother. Here Julius was, filthy dirty, in her home with beautiful furniture. She draped towels over her chairs, took out her beautiful china plates with flowers, placed the cheese burgers on the plates, sat Julius down, and said firmly, "Now we shall eat like civilized people!"

David Metzger

Every citizen in Salem, Oregon, should know the name David Metzger. Even folks here who have no use for music or Disney movies must have heard of David, because in our fair, frumpy town, he may be the closest thing to a celebrity.

Isn't it odd that Metzger has lived in Salem for nearly thirty years, and for most of that time, he has maintained a thriving business making music for Hollywood movies? His profession is straightforward: once a *cue* (the music for a scene) is signed off, he takes that cue, whether it is his own composition or that of another and orchestrates it into a demo for a recording session. He has a state-of-the-art studio, which I don't begin to understand, where he uses sophisticated software and a sound system for his orchestrations. A video monitor on the wall allows him to integrate his orchestrations to the direction in a movie or Broadway play. He has done compositions and orchestrations for sixty movies along with stage productions, television shows, movie shorts, even video games. He received two Tony Award nominations for music for his work on Broadway. He orchestrated all the music for *The Lion King*, which has been running on Broadway for more than twenty years and he orchestrated some of the music for the film *Frozen*. He is sought after not only because he produces good material but because he can do it efficiently and works well with other people.

Metzger explained to me how his work has been changed by technology.

> Twenty years ago, when I provided music for *Tarzan*, I did the score by hand. The piece was for the orchestra from the beginning;

there were no demos at all. Back in the old days, if there were any changes to be made, I had to do them on the spot while the orchestra was sitting there. I still have to do that sometimes even with all the demos. I get to the recording stage, and the director may say, "That is not quite right," and while the orchestra is sitting there, I am scrawling, trying out different ideas. There are always copyists on hand, people who take the score and make them into parts for the individual musicians. That happens sometimes, but in the old days, I could tie up an orchestra for extended periods of time. It would take about twice as long to record a movie as it does now. The process was labor-intensive, but it was more directly musical and easier to describe. Today, it has expanded to a much more complicated system and harder to explain. Now there are less talented people who can get in and make a living if they are good salespeople and know how to manipulate the samples.

For the movie *Frozen*, someone had an idea and wrote the story. I arranged the songs and orchestrated about a third of the score and two of the underscores (music played quietly under dialogue). I did not compose the songs—Bobby and Kristen Lopez, a husband-and-wife team, did that. They are not just incredibly talented but fantastic people to work with. Bobby writes a piano part, I take that part, and what you hear are the songs I have orchestrated. Bobby knows how to orchestrate himself, but he will give me his piano part to do sequencing—another term for this kind of program—and I will make him a demo on Cue Base (the software). You could say I do the mockup in the computer of what he has in mind for the orchestra and send a recording of that to Bobby and to the directors of the film. Everyone then gives comments on what they don't like or might want different, and I make the changes and send out another version. Some parts are spot on right off the bat, but occasionally there will be things they will want done a little differently.

This could go on up to when the orchestra comes in, but it rarely does, especially in animated films. The animation process takes so long; they have to animate the character's mouth to singing words. They need the songs to be locked down nine months ahead of the recording sessions, six to nine months. They animate to my demo. Once the animating to the demo is signed off, I don't touch it except to orchestrate it for instruments. It really doesn't change until the recording session. On *Frozen*, the recording session—I don't remember exactly—but I think there were five days of recording the songs.

The musicians are incredible. They are all sight-reading. They don't see the music until they sit down, but they have seen it all. They get there in the morning, kind of look through the folder to see if there is anything really nutty that might take a little practice and when the cue gets called up, they play, and that is the first time they have played through it. My experience has been the first time through, they play about 90 percent perfect, the second time 95 percent perfect, and the third time always perfect. It is not like rehearsing, because they start at the beginning and play all the way through. Maybe the trombones are a little behind the beat and they can do what is called punching in where there is a really tricky spot, or the rest of the piece is really good except for these few bars, and they can go in and record just a few bars that can be edited together to make a complete take, but the musicianship is incredible. I will be sitting there writing stuff and think, Can this really be played? I have twenty-six to thirty-two bar lines, very complicated, and are they going to play that tight together? I worry about it, and then I get to the recording stage, the piece comes up, and they breeze through it like it was nothing. The biggest joy of my job is getting to hear that level of musicians playing.

The difference with Broadway is that those folks play the same music night after night. They are equally incredible, but Broadway is a different world. What I admire the most is that they play eight shows a week, like *The Lion King*, which I orchestrated, which has been running on Broadway for twenty years now, so eight shows a week for fifty-two weeks a year for twenty years! They can sub out. They don't have to play every single show, but there are a number of musicians who are in the original orchestra. To me, the ability to do that without going crazy is equally impressive, but of course most shows don't last that long. Most shows last six months to one and a half years.

Metzger grew up in Corvallis. His parents had no musical background; in fact, his father was tone deaf to the point that the only way he could recognize "The Star-Spangled Banner" was by the words. He couldn't recognize the tune at all. His mother didn't play any instruments or sing, but the one thing that she did—this was back in the days of records—was play records throughout the day. It was not uncommon for the family to listen to *West Side Story* or *The Sound of Music*. She played them often, even when Metzger was a young child. There was always music on; it just wasn't performance music.

When Metzger was five or six, his parents signed him up for piano lessons, because that was what middle-class people did. He had shown no interest in music. He hated piano lessons so much that he quit after six months, and his parents let him. He had the same experience with elementary music; basic music classes were held once or twice a week, taught by a music teacher assigned to the grade schools, and he hated that. He wanted to do sports. He said,

> You look at me now and it is laughable, but I wanted to play basketball or baseball. I remember a rehearsal with our fourth grade music teacher, Mrs. Terhune. I didn't want to sing, so I was mouthing the words. I didn't hate the class so much that I was thrown out, but she busted me; she went right up to my face and said, "You are not singing," so I started singing.
>
> Then, I was really, really lucky, and this is where I count my blessings. I am saddened for all the people like me who never had this opportunity. When I went to Highland View Junior High—which is now torn down—in the seventh grade, (junior high schools in Corvallis went from seventh through ninth grade), I signed up for a shop class, a wood shop class, which was full. The administrators blindly put me into the choir class at the junior high and I didn't want to do it. I talked to my parents the week before school when I got my schedule and I said, "I really don't want to do this choir class." They said, "Try it. You never

know, you might like it." I got in there, and lo and behold, the choir director was a woman named Joyce Eilers, who happened to be at that time one of the top composers of junior-high choral music in the country. She made more from publishing than her teaching job, I am positive of that, and she was a great teacher. We got into the first couple of weeks, and I started recognizing that I was enjoying it and that a lot of the music we were singing were songs she had composed. Somehow I recognized that as being neat and unique.

About Christmas time, I said to her that I would like to try to write something. I didn't really know what I was doing, but every day, we had sight-singing (sight-reading) and ear-training. I think I was wired for this kind of stuff to begin with, but it wouldn't have been discovered unless I had taken this class. I sat down—I think this was over Christmas vacation, I don't remember for sure—I wrote out the Jan and Dean song *Barbara Ann* and thought this song would be fun to do. I wrote out a four-part harmony version and took it in to her and she must have seen something. No other kid would do that—very few kids would have done that—but I think I was wired naturally. I had enough ear-training and had seen the music in those first couple of months of seventh grade to correlate the pitches and rhythms on paper. Miss Eilers encouraged me completely to keep doing it. I would do more arrangements of pop songs like that and bring them in to her, and she would make little pointers.

I then started transcribing, which means listening to a record and writing out the musical instruments that you hear. By early eighth grade, my sister, who was a sophomore at Corvallis High School, had gotten into the band program, the jazz band in particular, and that stirred me to listen to big band records. I was listening to Buddy Rich, Count Basie, Woody Herman, Maynard Ferguson, Stan Kenton, and so on, and as I listened to those records, I could hear every voice. Somehow I could hear what the third trombone was playing. Of course, I wasn't as good at it then as I am now, because I was learning. I had been in music only a year, so I did that all the time. I still played basketball during basketball season, but that was about it. I became obsessed with this. I would do it for fun; I would sit there—this was back when there were records, so I would have to needle drop. When I got a little older, I used something like a cassette player, which didn't have as much clarity as a record but was easier to manipulate.

I did massive amounts of transcribing. Between Miss Eilers, her sight-singing, her encouragement, support, and ear-training, I got from fifteen minutes of sight-singing every day. That clicked for me. We would do pitch-training as well, and she would do interval-training. She would play a note and the next note, and we had to say what the interval was—a perfect fourth, a diminished fifth. I found that I had the ability to hear intervals. I don't have perfect pitch, but once I had a starting note, I could tell you any interval from there. That is how I transcribed things: these big band charts with five saxes, four trumpets and four trombones and I could hear the perfect way a band should sound. I am a horrible piano player and until computers came out in the 1980s, I would write everything down from my head straight to paper with no instruments to guide me.

In the eighth grade, because Miss Eilers was a great teacher, she would always, at least in rehearsals, have the choir read through and sing through music I had written. By the time I was in the ninth grade, she started having the choir perform music I had written for our concerts and festivals. It was arranging rather than composing, but honestly, I am a huge music education supporter, because without music educators like her, I wouldn't even have known about music. Who knows what my life might have been! My parents supported me, although they didn't understand it. They were unconditional in their support. I feel really lucky and am sad for those who didn't get the chance or have those opportunities.

When I went to high school, the band director at that time was Harvey Brooks. I am in debt to Harvey, along with Joyce Eilers, because when I switched over to band, Mr. Brooks picked up where Miss Eilers left off. When I was a sophomore, I was writing a lot of jazz band music in particular, and Mr. Brooks performed my pieces all the way through high school. A lot of the material the band would play was music I had arranged or transposed. If I had not had a band director as open to that idea of playing student arrangements, I wouldn't have gotten all the

> experience at that age when I was really young, developing the foundation that I was able to build on from that point on. There are band directors that wouldn't have supported me as much. I branched out to arranging concert band music, and by this time, I was composing original music and Mr. Brooks would play my original music. I saved him some money, but budgets weren't quite as tight then as they are now.

In high school, Metzger was involved in signature events that altered his life. He started dating Laura (his future wife) his junior year. They have now been married for thirty-five years (when I spoke with him). "She still runs the Boston Marathon," he said.

Eilers hooked him up with the Oregon State music department (Brooks supported it), and by his sophomore year, he was taking music theory at OSU. He said, "This gave me that much more background in traditional theory. Because of public school teachers, I had that great foundation."

Then at age sixteen, Metzger saw the first *Star Wars* movie. "When I saw *Star Wars,* I knew I wanted to do music for films. I was attracted to the combination of visuals with music. I was really focused."

He would not provide movie music for some time.

> You have to be three things: be assertive, be a people person, and talented. I think I have two of those three qualities. The one I didn't have is to be aggressive. I am not a salesman, not a self-promoter or marketer, and partly that is why I do the work of a composer but have never made that leap to being known as a composer. I am known as an arranger and orchestrator. I never made phone calls to people, never promoted myself, never did that kind of thing, but those are the people who get further along. I am a big people person, easy going, people trust me and know that I am going to get the job done. They like working with me; I am not a diva. There are other people in my field who are very egotistical and others don't like to work for those people. If I were being hired, who would I want to work for? Someone who is easy to work for or someone who is a jerk? Assuming the quality of the work will be the same. I do an okay job of working with people.

You have the perfect combination like Bobby and Kristen Lopez, who are extremely talented, really great people persons but are aggressive enough to put themselves out there without being jerks about it. They are not afraid to promote themselves, although I think that word is too strong. I was always afraid to call people up on the phone. I was raised to be humble; my parents were very Methodist. Don't bring attention to yourself. Be polite. I love that, but that did hold me back a little. I advanced myself by being a people person and I delivered a good product as long as people were willing to give me a chance. I climbed the ladder, but I didn't backstab up the ladder and because of that, I was helped out by people.

In college, I started working in Long Beach. I would network but not in an aggressive way. I started by working on promotional films. I would be called for jobs, but I had phone phobia; if I received phone calls, I wouldn't return them until five days later when I got the courage to return the call and at that point, the job was gone. I shot myself in the foot when I was climbing the ladder. Now I realize just out of politeness you need to return phone calls.

I think that I had a strong foundation when I was in my teens. I believe in the ten-thousand-hour thing: you put in ten thousand hours, you get pretty good at it. I think I put in my ten thousand hours arranging and composing and by the time I was in my early twenties, I knew what I was doing to a degree if people would give me an opportunity. Friends in college would refer me to someone they knew who was looking for arrangements. As long as I returned the call to that person, they would like what I did and they would refer me on to the next person who was looking for someone to help them out, so I networked in a very mellow and unaggressive way.

While into my twenties, my wife was in medical school at USC, did all her training at Los Angeles hospitals both for internship and residency and of course she wasn't making any money because she was in training and she was doing that while I was trying to build my career. During that time, I worked for four years with the Ice Capades, an old ice skating show now long defunct. Wayne Bergeron hooked me up with Maynard Ferguson and I arranged for him for two years. I would also copy music for other composers; I had a jazz band chart publishing business to sell to high schools and colleges. I printed my own brochures and mailed them out. I also played bass at events like weddings and generally cobbled together a survival living.

When we were both thirty-one, my oldest son was born at the very same time my wife finished her training. I didn't really have anything to show at that point and she said she was moving back to Oregon—I could come if I wanted to. It really wasn't that harsh and at that point I couldn't really say no, because I didn't really have anything going on in LA that was compelling me to stay. I didn't really want to raise a kid down there and so we moved up here. About two weeks before we moved, I got a call from a friend of mine who had a casual band, which I played bass for. He had just been hired as the music supervisor for *The Tonight Show* at the time when Jay Leno had taken over from Johnny Carson. The Jay Leno band was a different makeup from Carson's, so they needed completely new music. It was a brand new band, no catalogue and because I had written charts for his casual band and he knew I was a writer, he asked me if I would be interested in writing arrangements for *The Tonight Show*. He didn't know I was moving to Oregon at that point.

I wrote five pieces that first week, sent them in; two were original compositions, and three were arrangements for Branford Marsalis, who was the leader of the band. He liked what I did and wanted more. I went into a rehearsal the last couple of days before I was supposed to move. I thought I had better tell them I was moving to Oregon. He asked, "They have fax machines in Oregon, don't they?" (this was before the internet) and I said, "I think they do," so when we first moved up here, the first five years we lived in Salem, I did about 250 arrangements and compositions for *The Tonight Show*, virtually all of them from Salem. We lived in another house before we moved to our present house. Again, I have been so lucky. If not for that timing, I would have had to sell real estate or something else. What else would I have done up here in music? I was never cut out to be a teacher. To do what I do, I would have had to live in Los Angeles and live there long enough to make those connections and have them follow me to Oregon.

I didn't have to travel too much during *The Tonight Show* days, but after five years, Bradford left, my friend was fired and I never made the personal connection with the new band director, Kevin Eubanks. All of a sudden I was out of a job again. Bradford was there about three years and I was able to keep going with the new guy, but my friend was the person in the office organizing everything. Once he was fired, there was no connection.

At that point, I was back to thinking, "What am I going to do now?" But literally within a month I was called by another friend in LA, when I lived down there, who was asked to orchestrate a film for a guy named Mark Mancina who was the composer for the film *Speed 2*. Not the good one but the sequel to *Speed* —it was all on a boat and a really bad, bad movie. I didn't know Mark at this point, but the friend asked if I would orchestrate some of the movie. I thought, *Yeah!* That is what I had always dreamed of doing: to work on movies. I had never done that and I ended up orchestrating maybe 40 percent of the movie. I went down for the recording session, met Mark, and he loved all the work that I had done. He and I hit it off, so I thought, This is great. Maybe I can orchestrate for a couple of movies. I was involved about three months total on that movie, off and on. About a month after they finished the recording, I got a call from Mark, who had just been hired by Disney to produce the music for the Broadway version of *The Lion King*. The orchestrator he had lined up to do that show had just quit, and none of the music had yet been orchestrated. Would I be interested in doing that? Of course! I had never done a Broadway show in my life, but I said I needed to talk to my wife. Mark said I would need to be in New York for two weeks; that was probably all it would be.

I told my wife who by now was a doctor at Salem Clinic—we had two young children at that point—and I said I would need to be gone for two weeks. She said, "You probably should do it." Lo and behold, the two weeks turned into six months! *I was gone for virtually six months!* Of course, the way it turned out, *The Lion King* has become the largest grossing piece of entertainment in the history of the world. Just the Broadway version has made more money than any movie in history, any other Broadway show, anything in the world. It has been running for twenty years. I was nominated for a Tony Award for best orchestration. It was this bizarre sequence of events, and from that point on, Mark and I became really good friends.

The Lion King project really solidified my career at that point. Part of my people skills is that I don't get flustered in tense situations. That helped. Other people would flip out, but I am pretty even-keeled. I just keep going, work really hard. I don't slack off. Since then and for twenty years, everything Mark has composed I have orchestrated. Mark was already established before *The Lion King*. He had done *Twister* and *Speed*; he was already a fairly high-level film composer at that point, but *The Lion King* certainly didn't hurt him. I have probably done twenty-five to thirty films with Mark, then six or seven years ago, I branched out. Mark had moved to Carmel, which was not really in the business center, so his career slowed down a little bit and at that point, I started accepting calls from other composers. Mark didn't mind that, because he didn't have any work going on. I started working for Allen Sylvestre and John Powell; I have done a lot of films for Powell.

Frozen happened about three and a half years ago. Disney called me up; they were looking for an orchestrator to work with Bobby and Kristen Lopez on *Frozen*. Of course, I didn't know anything about *Frozen*—no one knows about a big hit movie before it is released, because you don't know whether it is going to be a hit or not. I thought it would be a good opportunity to work with Bobby and Kristen and build the level I had with Disney before. They called, and we hit it off, the three of us: Bobby, Disney, and me. Disney has a music department. The former head was Chris Montana, and now it is Tom McDougal, but I knew both of those guys since *The Lion King*. Now everything Bobby and Kristen do I am involved in, but Mark's career picked up again. We together have done probably three or four movies. *Moana* was the last one (he showed me the score).

Now I am completely a lone eagle. It wasn't that way when I first moved to Oregon. Before the internet, there was one year when I traveled to Los Angeles for at least twenty-five round trips. Now I am flying to New York quite a bit, because that is where

Frozen is taking place. I have to go back for workshops and so forth. Travel is not as big a deal now, because both of my kids are in Boston going to school. My wife retired two or three years ago; she can come with me now. Traveling is enjoyable unless you do too much of it.

I am really lucky, because with most of my work, I feel like I have a lot of creativity. I am really conceptualizing, because everything beyond a piano part is conceptualized by me. I have to come up with all the countermelodies and other things. A few times I even get to go beyond that. I have a relationship with the Willamette Masters Chorus. Every two or three years, they ask me to write something; I have done three pieces for them. That is fun because it is literally a concert piece of music. So much of my music relies on being supportive, either in films or what is happening on stage. It is fun to write a piece of music for music's sake, something I don't get much of a chance to do. I am lucky to be booked up as I am. I don't have time to do the other stuff, the fun stuff, but I am looking forward to doing that again.

Orchestrating for films can be tedious. When you are orchestrating for a movie, you only have an opportunity to work between when the cue is signed off and the start of the recording session. This can sometimes be compressed down to one or two weeks where it is physically impossible for one person to orchestrate an entire movie. The producer will get teams of orchestrators—it might be as few as two—but I worked on one movie where there were ten orchestrators, because there is not physically enough time for one person to do the job. If the music is in postproduction, we get pushed back until we are the last thing. You have the opening of the film and the deadline for the music to be finished, but if the filming gets pushed back a week, the music gets pushed back a week. If the editing gets pushed back two weeks, the music gets pushed back two weeks. The finish time or opening of the film never changes, but the amount of time for the music to be orchestrated could be down to one week between when the music is signed off and when they start recording. In cases like that, they have to bring in more bodies. Sometimes they will have co-orchestrators on the same cue, but I don't think that is a good idea, e.g., someone orchestrates the strings and another to something else. I have done the most co-orchestrating with John Thomas. Everyone gets assigned a cue, but John and I are pretty similar in our orchestrational style to the point that I don't know there is a big difference. We are pretty cohesive; our pieces fit together, but the only way the pieces get tied together is with the same orchestra. I can watch a movie and tell it was orchestrated by two or more people. Some movies are more cohesive than others.

Fortunately, when I am working with Mark or Bobby, I do everything myself. The whole conceptualization—mocking up the demo through the orchestration, my being on the recording stage to producing the recording—is all me. Every minute or second of that film has been processed by me. That is the most cohesive way. I don't like the concept of multiple orchestrators; films that are put out just for commercial purposes tend to have multiple orchestrators. Involving computer-generated images always messes up the schedule and at that point, you hardly hear any of the music anyway because of ginormous explosions and the like. I am of the ilk that I would rather work on fewer films and be involved in every aspect of the film. I have turned down fifteen films this year already.

I don't like to mix traditional and digital music. With some approaches to film music, a demo will be made, electronic or computer samples will be kept, and then the director will record a live orchestra over the top of that and blend the two together. I am not a big fan of that sound; to me, it sounds thick and the dialogue can't speak through as much. I prefer a real orchestra, but I do use synthesizers if it is not recreating the sound of the orchestra (he showed me examples). It cannot be strings. It has to be its own sound, a texture that is a synthetic kind of thing.

I ran into bizarre combinations of instruments in *The Lion King*. The director of that was Julie Taymor, an incredible visionary. She wanted to have ethnic African instruments as much as possible, which meant that I had to learn instruments I would not have known about before. I had to research and be really educated in African rhythms, an approach to rhythm that is very different from the way a Western percussionist looks at it. Our ears hear it one way, but it is written in a different way than we normally think of. I wanted it to be authentic, artistic, and organic, not a Western rip-off. You do something because it has commercial value to it, but you want it to be as real as it can be.

I work with composers of all kinds: those who want it down to the last detail to others who say "Just take it away" to everything in between. For example, Allen Sylvestre is a real nice guy but an old-school composer. He still writes everything in sketch form: two stays for the woodwinds, two for the brass, four stays for the strings, a couple for percussion. He will write it out, and he has mostly orchestrated it himself. With John Williams (David never had the opportunity to work with him), his orchestrators don't have much to do, because he has generally orchestrated it himself. With Allen, I take his sketch and essentially transfer it to a full score. He is very specific in what he wants and he is an incredible composer. The other extreme would be people who just give me a piano part, and I conceptualize everything.

Orchestration in its purest form is transcription. You have a sketch that is very detailed and I just fill in some of the details. When arranging, I am only getting a piano part, and that piano part might be just one line without any harmonies. As an arranger, my job is to develop that. I may orchestrate my arrangement. With some films, I was just given the picture and assigned to be a ghostwriter. I was the composer. I got compensated financially, but my name was not listed as the composer. I hate doing that. I used to like it because it was a chance to compose, but I won't do that anymore.

We shifted the conversation to the Salem-Keizer School District. I asked Metzger how teachers with small budgets can find good music. He said,

You can take a gamble and commission composers to write new music, but how good is it? During the summers when teachers attend workshops, directors will read through pieces, but that doesn't answer the budget problem. New composers can be self-publishing—that is what I did when I was in my twenties with jazz bands—but there is a point when to subsidize the composition process and the arrangement process, people do need to be getting money. That is why we keep doing it.

Since I am focusing on Salem-Keizer, I had two sons go through the music program, both at Sprague. What I appreciate about Salem-Keizer is that kids at North or McKay have access to high-quality music education, something that is disappearing throughout the country. Music programs are being cut all over; we are lucky here that we have a tradition and strong community support for it. Look at Portland. It is a shell of what it used to be. There is not enough funding, but Salem-Keizer has kept music as an important, valued treasure the community is still willing to support financially. A small town in eastern Oregon has people who have to make tough choices. What are they going to support? They don't have a strong tradition for a strong music program, so music will be one thing that has to be cut. Portland schools went through that twenty years ago. I didn't know any of this when I moved to Salem. My wife had a job at the clinic and our parents lived in Corvallis. That is why we moved here, but the music program here has been an unexpected bonanza. My boys had incredible opportunities all the way through high school to study with Steve Nelson, the kind of teaching so few people get anymore. I am so thankful. In my own life, it was the public school—the teacher—that put me where I am now. Without them, I wouldn't even have known about music, so I am a big fan of public schools.

Tyler Spragg Jr.

Tyler Spragg is one of the nicest people you will ever know. If you have a conversation with him, he will take great interest in what you have to say. He will laugh at your jokes if they are lame. If your jokes are bedridden, headed for hospice care, he may still laugh because he cares about you. He genuinely cares about people in general.

Tyler graduated from Oregon State University-Cascades in Bend, Oregon, and is now the marketing man for a boutique hotel in Bend. He is perfect for the job: he is tech savvy, gets along with people, and is very conscientious. He is one of our grandsons and comes to see us when he is in town.

When he got his first job at Bentley's in The Grand Hotel in downtown Salem, he got along with his fellow employees. He worked his way up from busboy to expeditor (the person who communicates between the kitchen and the servers) and did room service—a fun job, he said, which connected him more to the hotel and the front desk. Greg McManus, the vice president of operations, got Tyler the job at Bentley's and because of his good relationship with McManus, he expressed interest in working at the front desk and eventually became the front desk manager. This began because Tyler's younger brother was on the same little league baseball team as McManus's son. Tyler's father talked to McManus about getting Tyler the job. It was a classic example of "who you know" or at least who someone knows.

When Tyler worked the night shift, the work was slow, and he had time to study for his classes at Chemeketa Community College.

By working, Tyler was determined to get his education without going into debt.

Even during the day, the job as desk clerk was usually not stressful. However, one day, Tyler was scheduled to work the swing shift. A severe storm began blanketing the city with snow at 1:00 p.m. Tyler was called in early, and from the time he arrived at 2:00 until 9:30, the phones never stopped ringing. He said, "Not everyone could make it in, so it was two of us with the general manager helping out." The hotel's 196 rooms were scheduled to be filled nearly to capacity earlier in the day, but people on the roads couldn't make it to the hotel and started cancelling reservations carte blanche. Within a few hours, it looked as if all the hotel rooms would be empty. But people in from out of town realized they couldn't leave Salem and called for reservations. In another two hours, the hotel filled up again. He said,

> It was a huge task but a lot of fun. I got a room myself, and most people stayed an extra night. Everyone cleared out on the third morning when the roads were good enough for travel. It was a huge challenge having everything ready. The housekeepers were going nuts; it was insane. I will never forget the constant ring. It wasn't until 9:30 when there were a couple of moments of peace. If I weren't doing anything, I could always answer the phone. I had to stay in communication with the housekeepers. I just made it happen. We had walkie-talkies to communicate back and forth. I made a conscious decision that I would not be able to answer all these phone lines; I would just have to do my best. Prioritizing was something I had to think about constantly, but I love a good challenge, and that was certainly a challenge. Seven and a half hours of phone calls.
>
> At the front desk, I did my best, and that was all I could control. I think there were reasons they gave me the supervisor position. I believe I did a good job there, was proud of the work I did, and was grateful for the opportunity to work with Scott Snyder, the general manager. It was a total pleasure; I learned a lot from him.

His experience at The Grand Hotel drew him into a hospitality career. He did not seek a career in music, but from a young age, he had an affinity. He said,

> My mother would play music really loud in the car. That was a point of contention. "Mom, it's too loud! It hurts my ears!" Still, my first memories are a strong connection with some of the songs she played. There was the *Six Pence None the Richer* song, *Kiss Me* I remember hearing and loving. I have a huge connection to that song. There was a song by Ever Clear called *Wonderful,* which I loved at a young age. I just took to what Mom was listening to. I just remembered it causing this whirlwind of emotions—I don't want to pigeonhole it by saying emotions—but I evoke a lot of feelings from listening to music. A huge part of my relationship with music is listening; that is where it started and I still listen. That is an important part of my life, absorbing and listening.
>
> When I was seven or eight years old, I was listening to Dave Grohl, the drummer for Nirvana and I looked at Mom and said, "Mom, I want to play the drums." She said, "Oh, okay." It was an out-of-nowhere sort of thing. I have not met Grohl; that is certainly on my list with all the projects Dave has been in. He is really an insightful guy, inspirational. He has this quote somewhere, "People nowadays need to be okay with not being perfect right away. Just jump in there and do it. Get a bunch of friends together, go into the garage, and just suck. You aren't going to be good for a while; you have to try and work at it anyway." I think Dave is a cool guy. That is what turned me on to drums in the first place and so I had my eye on that for a while. Also in third grade when I was in Maryland, I learned how to play the recorder, reading basic music. The recorder is a pretty simple instrument to play. That was where I had my first organized exposure to general music and choir. In the sixth grade, percussion was now available. That was my first experience with drums. That was the start of my real musicianship.

After the sixth grade in 2004, Tyler moved to Oregon and in seventh grade, he took a percussion techniques course with ten steps from Brett Randolph. He was also in intermediate concert band. He said,

I enjoyed the middle school experience and learned a ton. What was really great about percussion was unlike, say, a saxophone where you were learning just one instrument. I was learning rhythm and melody through the avenue of snare drum, bass drum, marimba, xylophone, timpani, and auxiliary percussion like tambourine, shakers, and all the rest.

Tyler was in Randolph's Symphonic band in the eighth grade.

We all had our niche of what we were best at. We were never pigeon-holed anywhere, but I was the main tympani person. That was my forte, but I enjoyed everything else and had some fantastic parts on the snare and marimba. My friend Dan Cuffe was the percussion section leader. He and I had a little band in high school, just the two of us. Dan played the guitars. We only performed for his mom.

In high school, there was a scheduling conflict. I wanted to be in band, but I was in seminary. I still could have been in band, but I wouldn't have been able to take any PE classes. I would have had to give up something else that I wasn't willing to give up in order to make it happen, so I forfeited my participation in band at that point, because band was the lowest priority.

However, Tyler had a drum set and was playing on his own. He was teaching himself, so it wasn't a forfeiture of music itself but of school music.

I wish there was a way to make that happen, but it just wasn't in the cards. I was never in school band, but I took piano lessons from my grandmother and played drums in the garage. I also talked to our neighbor several times. We were in constant communication, because she was annoyed by the sound.

By this time, Tyler met Brendon Loscar, who became his next music buddy.

He would come over, and we would learn cover songs together we both liked. Brendon was a guitarist. I would show him some new songs, he would show me something. We had been doing that since I was fourteen. He and I are currently housesharing; we are practicing songs for open mic next week.

From the end of high school until he went to Bend, Tyler was never in an official band, but he jammed with friends and played with all kinds of people and different sorts of music.

> We never had gigs around town. We would play at our house, had friends over, have other bands over, and we would "share the bill." We were nineteen years old and a band called Crater came over—I loved their sound, had a lot of fun, and became part of that band. I played drums and sang, we all sang. Another one of my current roommates and a close friend, Justin Florip, was in that band also.

Tyler started playing the guitar in 2012 when he was playing with Crater.

> I rented the basement from a co-worker, Judy Houser. I lived in that house in north Salem and that is where Crater really took off. Because drums and other percussion instruments are the hardest to transport around, all the band gear after a rehearsal was always left at Judy's house. When there was no band practice, I had all these toys at my fingertips and that is how I started playing the guitar.

In late 2012, when Tyler was still in Salem, he lived with two band buddies, Justin and Terrence Robinson, in Justin's family home. Justin's mother, Sandra Florip, had moved to Arizona and the three boys stayed behind, agreeing that they would make the mortgage payments. Because the house was expensive to heat, they decided that they would not heat it for the entire winter and with the money saved, they would purchase a mixer. Tyler said,

> Buying the mixer would be our reward, but it was insane. There was no carpet except on the stairs; the rest of the house was all hardwood floors, and it was a cold winter. Everywhere in the house we could see our breath. By late January, I was walking around the house wearing three or four sweatshirts and a blanket at all times. We did buy the mixer, but we did not make it through the winter. One day, I walked up the stairs and was absolutely sweating. What is going on? I walked back down, and as soon

> as I entered the living room, Justin said, "I'm so sorry. I couldn't take it anymore. I will pay for all of it." No one was going to pay for all of it; it was time. We needed to be normal human beings again, but we were ice elves for a while.

In 2015, five years after Tyler left high school, he moved to Bend. For a time, he was part of informal bands. There were all kinds of musicians coming through; some faces were more familiar than others.

> I sat in with many musicians. I was the house drummer, if you will, but what I love about musicians passing through—and they still do—is that a lot of them are instrumentalists, so we are able to flip flop. I can play guitar or bass.

Tyler helped form a fusion band called The Same Coin, and they started playing gigs right away.

> It is a fusion of primarily funk, some jazz elements, rock elements also, just about as much rock as jazz. George Clinton, the front man for Funkadelic and Parliament, said that funk is imperfect dirty jazz that has a complex upbeat rhythm, good as dancing music. I think our band does a great job of getting people up and dancing. It is a lot of fun, the transference of energy from the band to the crowd. People are dancing, just throwing that energy back. As the back and forth gets stronger, it becomes an increasingly better experience. I think of it as fuel: I play the beat, add some fuel, they start dancing, which adds fuel for me. That interaction is really neat.
>
> Music is an integral part of my life in many different ways for many different reasons. The ways are the multiple avenues of consumption: listening, watching performances, recording, playing by myself, jamming with friends. Having jam sessions with pure improvisation, collaborating to create something. These are some of the many ways I can be involved in music. On jam night, it is usually with different performers; I am playing with some talented musicians. My favorite band, based out of Bend, is Jive Coulis. We went to one of their shows, and they are super talented. We met them and I am looking forward to having a jam night with them. The front man, Eric Leadbetter, asked me

to drum for some upcoming shows. Their drummer will not be able to be there. I already know their material, because I am a huge fan. Eric is doing a side project as well, so I am really looking forward to playing with him. He is a fantastic musician, but there is plenty else going on in Bend.

Music is a way to release, to have an avenue to express myself. I always feel the quieter, introvertish way of thinking is more my nature and speaking may not always be there for me. I feel I can speak through music better than using English. For that reason, it is a beautiful, cosmic thing, communicating ideas and feelings through various instruments. There is also the community around it—I meet a lot of interesting people who are musicians wherever I have lived. Just the networking is another reason why music is so much a part of my life.

Doug Zibell

Doug Zibell (pronounced Zi-bell') is the principle reason I wrote this book. His was the classic case of a high school kid gone awry only to be reined in by a teacher—in this case, his choir teacher, Loren Wenz. Zibell had twists and turns beyond high school, but he always wanted to remember that choir teacher who was one of the greatest inspirations in his life.

Zibell grew up in northeast Spokane, a lower-middle-class area where most kids were headed for the sawmills or possibly a job with the railroad. Zibell was different; he loved school, particularly history. His lifelong dream was to attend Washington State University in Pullman.

His father, Herman, had decreed that all three of his children would go to college, but it was an unfunded mandate. He was the breadwinner in the family, and on his wages from Armour Meat Packing, making sausages and hot dogs, there was no way he could finance college for any of his kids. Aside from telling Doug he should get into higher education, he took no interest in Doug's academics. In fact, he took little interest in anything his son did.

When Doug got into choir and cross-country running, Herman never came to a concert or a cross-country meet, in which Doug was involved. Herman was a hunter/fisherman in his off hours and he had no time for academics, music, or sports. Doug's mother Lois wasn't much better. Doug remembered that she never came to his choir events until the final concert. She was pushed into it by her visiting sister and they came to the concert together. Lois told Doug she was surprised by how good he was.

Zibell had always been able to sing well. He had been in choir from the fourth grade, but in his sophomore year at Rogers High School, he faced a choir teacher who had taught there for many years—had even taught Doug's mother—but he was nearing retirement and going through the motions. Zibell became fed up with choir and wanted to drop out. He had been in sports, but that wasn't going well either. He entered high school at five foot two and 100 pounds, and he was on the small side throughout his sophomore year.

By his junior year, Zibell became disillusioned with school and quit all extracurricular activities. Part of the problem, of course, was his unhappy home life. Despite his negative mental state, he kept his grades up, and by his senior year, he had enough credits to graduate by Christmas. He just wanted to get out of high school.

At the beginning of the year, his best friend, Rick Wise, approached him and said, "Doug, we have a new choir director. He is young, energetic—you have to meet him." Zibell told him that he had heard all this before, but Wise kept after him and finally he agreed to meet the teacher, Loren Wenz.

When they met, Wenz took Zibell to a back room and said, "Let's see how high and low you can sing." Zibell kept going up, and when he got to the high register, he could still hit notes without going into falsetto. Wenz was stunned. When he asked Zibell to go low, Wenz found that he could also sing bass, but he told Zibell that he needed a first tenor and he would be it.

Soon afterward, Wenz told Zibell he wanted him to be in his Shivesen Pop Choir. At the time, the concept of a pop choir was a relatively new phenomenon in Spokane. Only one high school had a pop choir the previous year, but Wenz and the directors from the other high schools wanted to get on board. Zibell had to audition, but he easily passed and made it into the pop choir. Wenz told him, "We have a concert in nine days. The pop choir is going to sing six songs and if you can learn them, you can sing." By this time, Zibell was on the cross-country team and tutoring fellow students and he didn't have the time to learn the music.

When he watched the pop choir perform, he thought, *I should be up there!* Afterward, Wenz came to him and said, "This will be the last concert you will ever miss, right?" Zibell said, "Yes sir! I will learn my music."

With Zibell in tow, the pop choir performed often, singing around the city. By January, it was ready for the Battle of the Pop Choirs, a true competition held at a high school in Spokane. The choir sang *My Sweet Lord* by George Harrison, *Close to You* by the Carpenters, and the song that got everyone going, *Aquarius (Let the Sunshine In).* Rogers High School got a standing ovation and won the contest.

Zibell thought Wenz was the first person who really believed in him.

Despite his range, Zibell never thought of himself as a soloist, because he didn't have much vibrato in his voice, but he could carry a tune well and didn't get stage fright with a microphone. Wenz worked with him to become a soloist and gave him an important lesson. He said, "At some point in your life, you will be singing solo and your mind will blank out. Just know it is going to happen. It happens to everyone."

Zibell asked, "What do I do?"

"Whatever you do, don't stop!"

"But what if I can't remember the words?"

"Doug, your brain will know the notes. It will tell you what notes to sing, but sing whatever words come into your mind. Just keep going, and you will get back on track. There is nothing worse than when you forget the words and you stop. The audience feels bad and they only look at you because they feel bad for you. The audience may not know the words, but they know the song and at any rate, they are going to feel bad, and you are going to feel bad. Then you have to start over, so don't stop."

Spokane had a Lilac Festival (similar to the Portland Rose Festival). Each high school nominated a princess who competed to become queen for the Lilac Parade. The Rogers High pop choir was asked to sing for the Lilac Coronation. It was the last group to sing with the song *My Sweet Lord*. Zibell had sung the song hundreds of times in his car and he knew it forwards and backwards.

Zibell sang the lead, the other choir members singing "hallelujahs" in the background, but in the second verse, his mind went blank. His mind was racing, trying to think of the words, but he remembered what Wenz had said: "Don't stop!" He started singing whatever words came to his mind, got back on track, and finished the solo. When they were done, Wenz said, "Changed the words for the second verse?" Zibell's girlfriend was sitting in the audience and she said, "Doug, I have never heard the second verse like that."

Zibell planned on going to college. He wanted to be a history teacher, but he had little hope that he could afford to attend. In a PE class during his senior year, the kids were doing presidential physical fitness exercises. One of the requirements was that they run all the track events (measured in yards in those days): the 100, 220, 440, half mile, mile, and two mile. Except for the 100 and 220, Zibell defeated everyone in his class. In the mile and two mile, his times were better than the members of the cross-country team. He joined the cross-country team and, in his first four meets, won all four races. Wenz looked on and told him, "You have a future here."

The cross-country team had an assistant coach, Rick Riley, who had graduated from Washington State University. When he saw Zibell win his fourth cross-country race, Riley told him, "Doug, next spring, if you run a 4:20 mile, I guarantee you will get a full ride at Washington State." In his second race in the spring, Zibell ran 4:18.5. He was going to the college he wanted to attend all his life, and his father was "thrilled beyond words." But when he visited the WSU campus, he found that some of the classes he would take would be in rooms with two to four hundred kids. He thought, How can I get a decent education under these circumstances?

When he told Wenz, his teacher asked, "Have you considered Whitworth?" Whitworth was a small, liberal arts school at the north end of Spokane. Zibell had not considered Whitworth because it was impossible financially. At that time (1971), the total cost of going to WSU would be $2,000. Attending Whitworth would be double that, and unlike WSU, he would be entering with no athletic scholarship. It was impossible. He didn't think he was good enough to run in college anyway.

Wenz said, "Why don't you check it out? Just trust the Lord. If you are meant to go there, you will get it worked out."

Wenz set up a meeting for Zibell and two classmates from the choir with Dr. Milton Johnson, who had been Wenz's advisor when he went to Whitworth. When the boys auditioned for the traveling choir, they passed and Johnson said, "I will give each of you a $1,000 scholarship, but you have to be a music major." That was fine with Zibell and his friends. Because of his good grades in high school, Zibell received an additional $2,000 in scholarships, but he was still $1,000 short for attending and staying on campus.

When Zibell visited the financial aid office, the officer looked at the name and said, "Zibell—didn't you run for Rogers High?" As luck would have it, at that moment, the cross-country coaches came walking down the hall. The aid officer asked them, "Do you folks have an extra thousand dollars in your pockets? I have a boy here who will be on your cross country team."

One coach said, "I don't think he can make it. I am bringing in four all-staters from California, but he can try out." He turned to Zibell, "Come down to the track right now. If you can run a 4:20 mile, I will give you the thousand bucks."

Zibell had not been running all summer and was out of shape, but when he got to the track, he ran into one of seniors on the team, Bob Isitt, who graduated from Rogers High. Isitt told him, "Stick with me. I will get you through this." He gave Zibell his first pair of running shoes: Adidas Gazelles. (Before that he had run on Converse, which were regular gym shoes.) Zibell ran his first three laps, and Isitt called out, "Now give it all you got!" Zibell ran the mile in 4:19.5 and received his third scholarship, affording him attendance at Whitworth.

There was one huge problem: track and choir practices were scheduled in the same time slot. Zibell was one of the top five runners and one of only two tenors who could hit the high notes in the first performance of *Jesus Christ Superstar*. He tried to solve the problem by splitting the difference, giving both activities half his time. He worked out at cross-country and went to choir practice without taking a shower, but he had both coach and teacher mad at him.

After the fall semester, Johnson took Zibell aside and said, "You have to make a choice: music or running. You can do the next semester, but I have to have someone I can count on." Zibell told him he understood. He would love to have been in music, but he had not learned to read music very well. He would have to pass a piano proficiency test and he didn't know how to play the piano at all. After the first year, he had to drop music.

Zibell would be losing a thousand, but he picked up a thousand because the track coach realized how good he was. Zibell remembered that Wenz encouraged him to attend Whitworth, and he still thinks it is one of the best decisions he ever made.

It just so happened that Wenz was the choir director at Knox Presbyterian Church. He said, "Why don't you come and sing with us?" Zibell was working at a local grocery store more than twenty hours a week, but he was able get Wednesday evenings off for choir practice. His cross-country mates didn't have to work—they got money from parents or grandparents—but Zibell had to work to pay for books, insurance, and meals. At the end of the week, if he had ten dollars in his pocket and a full tank of gas in his car, he thought he was rich.

After choir practice on Wednesday nights, Wenz invited some of the kids to come over to his house and talk. Not that Wenz had answers to any problems, but he was happy to sit there and listen. For the last three years Zibell was at Whitworth, he was in the Presbyterian choir because, as he says, "Loren made music fun."

After graduation, Zibell lost track of Wenz for many years. Zibell moved to Portland, eventually forming his own company selling products to grocery stores. In 2001, his old friend, Rick Wise, called and suggested that all thirty-three charter members of the Shivesen Pop Choir get together for a thirty-year reunion. Both started making phone calls, and many of the former members said they would come if Wenz would be there. Zibell was assigned to call Wenz, who was by then was living in Salem. Wenz said he wasn't keen on doing it. Wenz's wife, Jenna, got on the phone and said, "Loren doesn't like reunions." Zibell said, "But we were his first choir, his first baby. We would really like you guys to come." She said, "Let me work on it." Later, she called back and said, "Okay, we are coming."

In July 2001, twenty-seven former members of the pop choir met in a basement of a large church and the kids, now adults, were going to do some singing. Zibell brought a bunch of sheet music, but Wenz said, "As much fun as it would be to do that, I just want to know about you guys." They sat around in a circle. Zibell said it was wonderful to catch up on peoples' lives.

Afterward, Wenz came up to Doug and thanked him for arranging the reunion. He thought it was a lot of fun. Initially, he said he would lead the pop choir, but then he said, "I'm just about the people. That is fine."

Wenz taught at South Salem High School for twenty-one years and then taught part time at George Fox University thirty-five miles north of Salem. Zibell came to a few Christmas concerts and when Wenz held his final concert at George Fox, retiring for good, Zibell and many fellow choir members from Rogers High surprised him by being in the audience. Wenz said it was the best present they could have given him.

Zibell and his wife, Dianna, had a son and daughter: both had muscular dystrophy and passed away at a relatively young age (a third daughter was born later). Their son, Richard, was tone deaf but brilliant. He went to Oregon State University for a year, but when he was a junior, his sister died, which put him into a depression. He was in a wheelchair and in declining health. He told Doug that before he died, he wanted to go to an Ivy League school. He was admitted to Harvard and went there for one year, getting around in a wheelchair, but then he said he wanted to come home—that was where he wanted to die. Doug and Dianna had three wonderful years with him before he passed away.

Zibell said that his daughter, Brynne, had a voice like an angel. Early on, she could sing harmonies and they sang many harmonies together. She played the flute in the Centennial High School marching band, sitting in a motorized wheelchair in neutral as Doug pushed her around.

A couple of weeks before Brynne passed away, she asked her father, "Is it better to go quickly or linger as I am doing? Her lungs were becoming weaker; she had phlegm in her throat and couldn't cough it up. One day, she was having trouble breathing. She yelled to her dad to come down from his office. She was with her favorite nurse when he arrived. Brynne said, "Daddy, I am going to die now." Doug said a prayer: *Please don't let her suffer, don't let her suffocate!* He believes to this day that the Lord was reaching out to her and she went peacefully. She was only seventeen.

She had often heard her father talk about Wenz and said, "Daddy, I wish I could have had him for a choir teacher." Zibell says she would have loved it, but she never had the opportunity to meet him.

As for Wenz, at the last Christmas concert at George Fox, he told Doug, "I use you as an illustration at the start of each year with the new choirs that I have. With guys especially, I say, 'This kid couldn't read music, but he had an ear, and no matter what I asked him to sing, he could adapt to it. He had the confidence to hit that note. If you work at it, you can do that too. What was his name? Doug Zibell. Doug, you are the one! You were the one I was talking about."

Zibell said, "I can't reach those high notes like I used to."

Wenz said, "You don't have to have all the ability in the world, but if you believe in yourself, trust your abilities and trust in what

I am teaching, you can do that."

Zibell had no idea that Wenz was using him as an example all those years.

He still sings in church choirs. His favorite concert is Christmas, because he loves Christmas music, especially *Silent Night*. When Zibell sings in a choir, he sings first tenor or bass. He still has that range.

Acknowledgements

ALL INFORMATION IN THIS BOOK WAS SUPPLIED BY THE PERSON featured in a mini-bio with the exception of the anecdote on Katie and the piece on Pamela Miller. The Katie story was supplied by Ben Stokes, band teacher at South High School in Salem. The information on Pamela Miller was provided by two friends plus information from Miller's funeral. Two people played a minor role in the bio on Jim Taylor.

I want to thank all those people whose bios are within the pages of this book. I talked in person or spoke by phone to the following people: Cheyenne Hayes, Dick Withnell, Juan Valdez, Julie Rundquist, Jim Taylor, Michael Swan, Diane Swan, Ryan Swan, Caitlin Swan Clark, Walt Farrier, Randy Kem, Nicole Elwell, Lindsey Gellenbeck, Jennifer Lewis, Steve Phillips, Marti Bowles, Cynthia Richardson, David Metzger, Tyler Spragg Jr. and Doug Zibell.

I also want to thank Connie Snyder and Karen Kohne who gave me a large percentage of my information on Pamela Miller and I appreciate permission from Carolyn Alexander and Julius Liang to draw information from the funeral. For additional information on Jim Taylor, I want to thank Leah Garro, office manager at Claggett Creek Middle School and former chair of the McNary High School choir booster club; and Andy Thomas, former choir teacher at Whiteaker Middle School in Keizer who now teaches at McNary High School. I want to thank Ben Stokes for giving me the anecdote on Katie.

I also want to thank the team at Luminare Press for making this book possible: Melissa Thomas and Claire Last for designing the book cover and layout of the text, Kim Harper-Kennedy for keeping my project moving in a timely manner, Lori Stephens for her very helpful editing, and finally owner Patricia Marshall for taking me on to begin with and her special inspiration to turn my product into two books instead of one.

—Frank Spragg

37108923R00095

Made in the USA
San Bernardino, CA
27 May 2019